QUALITY CERTIFICATION FOR THE SMALL BUSINESS: AN IQA GUIDE

QUALITY CERTIFICATION FOR THE SMALL BUSINESS: AN IQA GUIDE

ALAN A GRIFFIN

Published for The Institute of Quality Assurance by

SYDNEY JARY LIMITED
9 Upper Belgrave Road   Clifton   Bristol   BS8 2XH   England

First published September 1994

Edited by Lois Jary
© Text and charts/tables copyright Alan A Griffin
Cartoons by Hodges Associates
© Copyright Alan A Griffin

A catalogue record for this title is available from the British Library

ISBN 0 9512078 5 7

All rights reserved. No part of this publication may be reproduced, stored in a retrieval system, or transmitted in any form or by any means, electronic, mechanical, photocopying, recording or otherwise, without the prior permission of the publishers.

Designed, produced and typeset in Times New Roman by
AVONWORLD LIMITED
PO Box 568, Bristol BS99 1PZ

Cover: Photography by Cotters Photography, Kingsdown, Bristol
Colour reproduction by Black Cat Graphics, Portishead, Bristol

Printed and bound by Bookcraft Ltd, Midsomer Norton, Bath, Avon

ACKNOWLEDGEMENTS

The publishers would like to express their thanks and appreciation to the following companies for granting permission to photograph and/or use shots included in the composite photograph on the cover:

- M J Rees & Company Ltd, Almondsbury Bristol
- Ollis Transport Ltd, Avonmouth Bristol
- Bristol Industrial Engraving, Bristol
- Strachan & Henshaw Ltd, Bristol

and to SGS Yarsley International Certification Services Limited and Mr John Feltham of Warsash for permission to reproduce his Quality Assessment Certificate and Schedule on page 3.

The Author

Alan A Griffin has over 35 years' experience of quality management in small and medium sized businesses. He is a Fellow of the Institute of Quality Assurance and is currently Chief Executive Officer of Alan A Griffin & Associates, who have an established international reputation for the provision of Quality and Environmental Management Training and Consultancy in a wide range of manufacturing and service industries.

The Institute of Quality Assurance (IQA)

The Institute of Quality Assurance was founded as the Technical Inspection Association in 1919, incorporated in 1922 as the Institution of Engineering Inspection and granted its present title in 1972. It has since its formation been the only professional body or learned society in the United Kingdom whose sole purpose is the promotion and advancement of Quality practices and whose qualifications for individual membership are knowledge and experience in that subject.

The Institute's principal aims are

- To seek the advancement of quality management and practices and to facilitate the exchange of related information and ideas.

- To promote the education, training, qualification and continuing professional development of people involved in quality assurance and management for quality.

- To provide a range of services to members and, where appropriate, to the community at large.

Quality is now recognised to be everybody's business, not just the Quality practitioner's, and consequently the Institute has widened its interests to embrace all the human and organizational considerations implied by the phrase *Total Quality Management.* The practice of Quality is therefore relevant to all industrial, commercial and public sectors, to all functional departments within them, and to all working levels.

Quality Certification for
the Small Business:
an IQA Guide

CONTENTS

Author's Preface		xi
Foreword		xiii
Chapter 1	Introduction	Page 1
Chapter 2	Requirements of the Standard	13
Chapter 3	Quality Manuals & Procedures	35
Chapter 4	Implementing the Documented Quality System	49
Chapter 5	Control of Measuring and Test Equipment	59
Chapter 6	Effective Quality Control Records	65
Chapter 7	Internal Audits and Management Reviews	69
Chapter 8	The Assessment & Registration Process	85
Chapter 9	Preparation for Assessment	101
Chapter 10	Maintaining the Quality System Post-Registration	107
Appendix A	Glossary of Terms relating to Quality Concepts with a list of the International Quality Standards and their BS 5750 equivalents	111
Appendix B	Useful Addresses	117
Index		xvii

AUTHOR'S PREFACE

1994 re-classification of Quality Standards

It should be noted that the 1994 issues of British Standard BS 5750 Parts 1, 2 and 3 are now titled

> BS EN ISO 9001: 1994
> BS EN ISO 9002: 1994
> BS EN ISO 9003: 1994

respectively. However, for reasons of general familiarity in small businesses, I have, at least in the first edition of this book, continued to refer to BS 5750 Parts 1, 2 or 3 as appropriate. A list of the BS 5750 parts and their new equivalents is included in Appendix A — see below.

Glossary of terms and organization names and addresses

A glossary of terms relating to quality concepts appears at Appendix A starting on page 111 and a list of useful names and addresses at Appendix B starting on page 117: I have tried to include all relevant organizations and government departments which are referred to in the text.

Alan A Griffin
Hayling Island
August 1994

FOREWORD

BY PAM MACALESTER
CHAIRMAN, WESSEX REGION,
FEDERATION OF SMALL BUSINESSES

WE IN the Wessex Region of the Federation of Small Businesses are delighted to have the opportunity to write a foreword to this guide, commissioned by the IQA and written by Alan Griffin.

Alan is a supportive member of our organization who has always been prepared to help fellow small business people faced with the dilemma of what to do about BS 5750. Often they have been presented with a situation whereby major customers impose on them the need to gain certification almost as a licence to trade! To the uninitiated, the prospect of what appears to be a minefield of difficulties and potential cost has frequently been a serious deterrent and an unwelcome addition to the many problems of running a small enterprise in today's seemingly unending welter of regulation.

Alan's calm professional guidance has soothed such fears and — for many an owner of a small enterprise — removed the uncertainty of how to prove that he or she has a 'quality' business.

It is a great satisfaction to us to know that the help which Alan has given to us in Wessex will now, through this book, be available to a much wider audience of small and medium sized businesses, and we are confident that they will benefit as we have done from his sound knowledge of the subject, his years of experience, and his good sense.

"Quality? Couldn't afford it"

Chapter 1

INTRODUCTION

SINCE 1985, when accredited certification to the quality standard was introduced, over 30,000 UK businesses have been assessed and registered to BS 5750* and its international equivalent, ISO 9000.

Although these standards have enjoyed unprecedented worldwide acclaim from the international business community, the management of many small businesses in the UK and the rest of Europe are still very dubious of the benefits of adopting them as a model. They much prefer simply to continue to do business in their own way, as though effective management is a skill that all entrepreneurs are born with, which therefore comes naturally to them without any conscious effort on their part. This illusion persists in spite of the daily evidence around them of small businesses failing to meet their modern-day customers' needs, and hence failing to survive. It is so much easier for them to go along with the media and blame the economy or Government policies, than to make the effort to take a fresh look at their own style of management — which should be a means not only of survival but also of continuing improvement for the 1990s and beyond.

However, for those small and medium-sized enterprises — SMEs — whose management are prepared to consider a change of style, this guide has been prepared to clarify just what is required of them in establishing an effective quality management system (QMS) based on the requirements of BS 5750/ISO 9000*.

Before we can do this, however, we should define exactly what we

---

* Now re-classified BS EN ISO 9001, 2 and 3: 1994. See Author's Preface on page xi mean by 'small' and 'medium' enterprises.

Generally, a 'small' company is one which has fewer than 50 employees, total assets below £1.5 million, and an annual turnover of less than £3 million. This definition applies to over 95% of all businesses operating in the UK and therefore this guide is primarily aimed at this size of business, rather than at the larger 'medium' enterprise, which has been defined as having between 50 and 500 employees, assets of up to £6 million, and an annual turnover of £11 million or more.

In total, SMEs account for some 99% of businesses in the UK, with the smaller companies in general acting as the suppliers, subcontractors and service providers to the medium enterprises, who in turn service the needs of the major purchasing agencies in both the public and private sectors. Between February 1988 and June 1994 the DTI has given quality consultancy assistance to no less than 40,000 SMEs.

It is, however, the major organizations, in both public and private sectors of the national and international markets, which have had the foresight to realise the potential benefits to the entire organization, if top management have a positive policy towards quality. It is these organizations which now increasingly insist that their own suppliers and subcontractors should demonstrate a similar commitment to the principles of BS 5750/ISO 9000.

The practices of management suitable for the larger organization are obviously totally different from the methods adopted by the average small business. However, all organizations, irrespective of size, have one common objective: to minimise unscheduled costs. Only by taking positive steps to prevent problems, and the costly additional work required to correct them, will they be able to survive in increasingly competitive markets. Mistakes cost money and can result in dissatisfied customers and loss of profitability, which can soon become a vicious spiral towards bankruptcy.

The top management of any enterprise can always benefit from an objective reappraisal of their methods for the achievement of quality, and hence customer satisfaction and profitability. The BS 5750/ISO 9000 generic series of standards can be used for this purpose to the benefit of SMEs, in both the manufacturing and service sectors, regardless of size or type of product. Indeed, even one-person businesses have successfully demonstrated their compliance to these standards to the

Introduction

satisfaction of independent organizations such as one of the accredited certification bodies.

SGS Yarsley
International Certification Services Limited

ASSESSMENT SCHEDULE
93/2261

Company: John Feltham

SGS Yarsley
International Certification Services Limited

Certificate Number

93/2261

This is to certify that the
Quality Management systems of

John Feltham
Warsash

have been assessed and registered as meeting the requirements of ISO 9002 / EN 29002 / BS 5750 Pt 2

The scope of registration is detailed on the Assessment Schedule bearing this certificate number.

SGS Yarsley International Certification Services Ltd
Signed by

21 September 1993

Valid for three years subject to satisfactory surveillance

Registered Office:
SGS Yarsley
International Certification Services Limited
SGS House, 217/221 London Road,
Camberley, Surrey GU15 3EY.

Whilst all due care and skill was exercised in carrying out this assessment, SGS Yarsley ICS accept responsibility only for proven gross negligence. This is not a legal document and cannot be used as such. The use of the Accreditation mark shown on this certificate indicates accreditation in the respect of those activities covered by that Accreditation Authority. This certificate remains the property of SGS ICS to whom it must be returned on request.

NATIONAL ACCREDITATION OF CERTIFICATION BODIES

Registration Number
005

Member of the SGS Group (Société Générale de Surveillance)

QUALITY CERTIFICATION FOR THE SMALL BUSINESS: AN IQA GUIDE

As this guide will — I hope — demonstrate, establishing and maintaining an effective quality management system need not be a costly task for the small business. The secret of success is, as always, simplicity and the application of common sense to the needs of the business.

Even independent assessment and registration does not have to become an unacceptable burden. Many of the accredited certification bodies in the UK are now prepared to accommodate the needs of small businesses for less than the cost of a regular advertisement in their local newspapers: say £20 - £30 per week.

What is required, however, is both commitment and leadership from the top management within the organization. This is vital to ensure that the QMS exactly matches the requirements of their business: no more and no less.

Each QMS must therefore be unique to its own organization. BS 5750/ISO 9000 can be likened to the skeleton which the organization's management fleshes out to create a recognisable corporate image.

Management, particularly in a small business, must always be on their guard against 'overkill', which is all too often advocated by so-called 'consultants' who have neither hands-on management experience of small businesses nor in-depth knowledge of the practical application of system models such as BS 5750/ISO 9000.

We therefore dedicate this guide to all those 'entrepreneurs' who believe that quality is the prime means of survival in the 1990s.

Quality Management

What is it and why should SMEs have to be registered?

The formal definition of quality, as given in *BS 4778/ISO 8402 — Quality Vocabulary*, is:

"The totality of features and characteristics of a product or service that bear on its ability to satisfy stated or implied needs."

The formal definition of quality assurance is:

Introduction

"All those planned and systematic actions necessary to provide adequate confidence that a product or service will satisfy given requirements for quality."

It is this element of confidence that a purchased product or service will meet the stated or implied needs of the customer which has made an organization's possession of a certificate of registration to BS 5750 Part 1, 2 or 3 (ISO 9001, 9002, 9003)* so attractive to many purchasers. However, customer satisfaction is derived from a combination of many variables, and this requires management skills in the effective deployment of an organization's physical and human resources.

A quality management system could be likened to a tripod, which won't stand unless each of the legs is equally sound. Top management must likewise give equal attention to all three 'legs' of their QMS, in their overall business plan.

What are the three legs of the quality tripod?

1. CUSTOMERS

If the needs of the customers are not met in full, it is unlikely that the organization will receive the repeat business which is essential for sustained growth. Without satisfied customers, there can be no 'pay days'.

2. FUND PROVIDERS

One of the main objectives of any business is to create an acceptable return on capital invested. As it is usually the market place which determines the price of a product, business management must always be aware of each product's unit costs in order to maintain an acceptable level of profitability. Too many costly mistakes can quickly erode the return on capital invested.

3. EMPLOYEES

One of the greatest assets of any business is its employees. If correctly applied, BS 5750/ISO 9000 can ensure that all employees

---

* Now re-classified BS EN ISO 9001, 2 and 3: 1994. See Author's Preface on page xi

have a greater awareness of their company's policy and objectives, leading to greater job satisfaction. We all like to feel that our own contribution matters to our company's management, and that the company's products are seen by customers to be of acceptable quality.

A quality management system must never be allowed to become a constraint on the effective running of a business. A well designed and documented QMS is essential for any organization wishing to establish an effective system of management based on the philosophy of Total Quality Management (TQM), where the aim is to harness both the human and material resources in the most effective way to achieve all the company's objectives, including total customer satisfaction.

BS 7850 is the recommended reading for all those who wish to study this aspect of business management in more depth. Initially, however, the management of a small business should take time to read through the following guidance documents in order to gain a greater appreciation of what quality management is all about.

Manufacturing organizations:

BS 5750 Part 0:Section 0.2 — Guide to Quality Management and Quality System Elements

Service organizations:

BS 5750 Part 8 — Guide to Quality Management and Quality System Elements for Services

"But all these standards are expensive, and we cannot spare the time to study them!" many managers will say. Well, nobody ever claimed that it would be easy: there is no such thing as a 'free lunch' in the running of a small business. However, the initial outlay in time or money cannot be considered excessive compared with the potential benefits of gaining a better understanding of what effective quality management is really all about.

We can now begin to consider the true purpose of each of the three possible system models which can be used as the basis for the design

Introduction

and implementation of a company's QMS. The choice will, of course, depend on each individual company's needs in relation to its products and/or services.

BS 5750 Part 1 will apply when a company is fully responsible for the original design of the product as well as its manufacture, and — where applicable — the installation and servicing of its products after delivery to the customer. However, many organizations within the service sector also 'design' the service they offer to their customers, and should therefore consider Part 1 in conjunction with the guidance given in Part 8.

BS 5750 Part 2 is the standard most likely to apply to a small business which manufactures to established designs, either their own or those of their customers.

BS 5750 Part 3 can be used when it can be verified, by final inspection and test prior to delivery, that the customer's requirements have been fully met. In the case of simple products or services, compliance with this standard may be all that is required by small businesses in order to satisfy customer needs. However, in the UK, many of the established certification bodies appear to be reluctant to carry out an independent assessment and registration against it.

This brings us to the question of the need for independent assessment and registration. Unfortunately, this has been allowed to become almost an obsession with many companies within the UK, as witness the prolific growth of accredited certification bodies over the last two or three years! The BS 5750 standards, however, were not originally created solely for the purpose of assessment and registration, and an SME's management would be ill-advised to consider that the possession of a certificate is the ultimate goal.

How can an SME's management handle this situation? What are the options available if the maximum benefits are to be derived from BS 5750?

Firstly, it would be advisable for senior management to consider the following questions:

1. How can a close and effective working relationship be established and maintained with the company's major

customers? Is the organization seen by its customers as a 'caring company'?

2. Has an effective communication link been established which will ensure prompt and factual feedback to identify and resolve problems quickly, in order to prevent disputes arising?

3. How do customers choose their suppliers and/or subcontractors?

    a) By market reputation?

    b) By evaluation of sample products?

    c) By reliance on the judgement of third parties?

    d) By comparing price and delivery times?

4. How will customers evaluate the company's products/services?

    a) By on-receipt inspection and/or testing?

    b) By verification of predelivery inspection or test data, or evidence of process control records?

    c) By reliance on the integrity of the company's QMS, based on periodic audit of the company's quality management practices?

Only when these questions have been fully considered can the SME's management determine the value they place on an independent assessment and registration by a third party, such as one of the accredited certification bodies.

We must always remember that, although great benefit can be derived from the intelligent application of the standard, BS 5750 assessment and registration remains a matter for discussion and voluntary

INTRODUCTION

agreement between a company and its customers, although of course due regard must always be given to market pressures.

Until there is an acceptable alternative for small businesses, we must consider the question of where we can turn to for help in preparing ourselves for the almost inevitable visit by the assessors from one of the accredited certification bodies which offer their services within the UK. Remember the old Latin tag 'Caveat emptor' — 'Let the buyer beware'. The 'quality industry' is now, in spite of the current recession, one of the major growth industries, not only in the UK but on a worldwide scale. There are many people who will be only too pleased to take your money in return for very little benefit.

Unless you are already knowledgeable about quality management systems, you will need some help in modifying your existing working procedures and practices to bring them into line with BS 5750 requirements. There are two alternatives: either take time out to attend a training course or employ a consultant.

Training is possibly the most cost-effective method and there are many extremely good courses available, ranging from one to five days in duration. Recommended sources of information are as follows:

- The Institute of Quality Assurance
- Local Training and Enterprise Councils (TECs) and/or Chambers of Commerce
- Local Colleges of Further Education

The second alternative — using a consultant — should be handled with care. It will be helpful to seek advice from the nearest Business Link, the centre which offers a comprehensive package of services targeted to meet the needs of local business. Details of the growing network of Business Links are available from the Trade and Industry section of regional Government Offices. Note that different arrangements operate in Scotland and Wales.

Before engaging a consultant, always ask for — and take up — references, and make sure that the consultant has first-hand experience of your type and size of business. Beware of any who offer you a ready-prepared quality manual or package of procedures. It may prove at best to be an unacceptable constraint on your preferred working practices,

Quality Certification for the Small Business: an IQA Guide

and at worst to be an extremely costly bargain. Information on qualified consultants can be obtained from the British Quality Foundation (BQF) and the Association of Quality Management Consultants (AQMC), both of whom require their listed consultants to adhere to a strict Code of Practice.

An effective documented quality management system should be unique to the individual company. It therefore takes time to establish this system, if it is to be of any benefit.

What is all this likely to cost?

Even for a very small business, training and consultancy fees are likely to be in the order of £2000 plus, with a further £1000 to £2000 plus to be paid to the certification body of your choice. This is just for the initial registration. There will also be a further £500 to £800 plus to be found annually to cover the twice-yearly visits by the assessors to see if you are continuing to maintain your quality management system to the requirements of the standard.

Many of the UK certification bodies are now offering special low cost registration schemes especially designed for the very small organization of fewer than 5 employees. Typical costs as of June 1994 are £300 to £500 for the initial assessment, with a further £400 to £600 for the annual surveillance fees.

All told, this is a very expensive undertaking just to satisfy our customers! We need, therefore, to spend our money wisely. However, remember the old adage: 'If you pay peanuts, you can only get monkeys'.

INTRODUCTION

THE EVOLUTION OF QUALITY MANAGEMENT

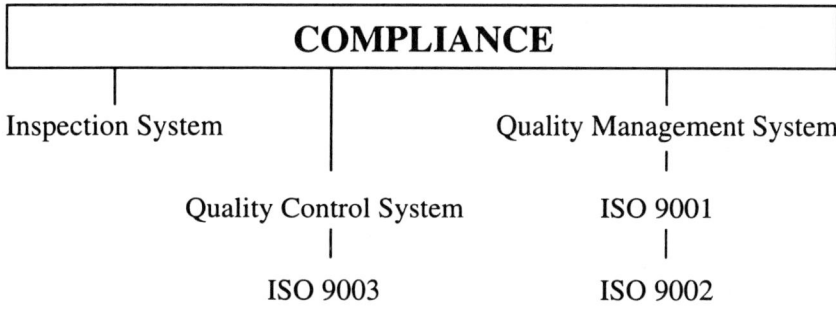

Chapter 2

REQUIREMENTS OF THE STANDARD

NO AMOUNT of external help, however professional, will guarantee your continuing survival in the increasingly demanding markets of the 1990s, unless you get to grips with the really effective management of your business.

Your future is in your own hands. Why not put aside just a little of your time to study BS 5750 and see exactly what it requires of you? If you don't already possess a copy, then go along to your nearest public reference library and ask to read through their copy. You will find that it is not the bureaucratic document that you may have been led to expect. It is a model of effective management practice which even the smallest family business can successfully apply.

Let us consider just one requirement:

Requirement 4.1   Management Responsibility

Ask yourself the following questions.

- Can we define what we mean by quality?

- Have we really thought through exactly what our policy on quality is?

- Have we set any objectives in respect of quality?

- Can we demonstrate our commitment to quality?

- Have we written all this down so that everybody in the organization can read and understand it?

- Do we have a formally defined organization where everyone has a clear understanding of his or her individual responsibilities and authorities?

- Has a management representative been appointed with defined authority for ensuring that the quality system fully complies with the requirements of the chosen systems model — BS 5750 Parts 1, 2 or 3?

- Does the management team periodically and formally review the suitability and effectiveness of the adopted quality system?

- Do we keep records of the findings of such reviews and their follow-up actions?

If the answer to any of these questions is No, ask yourself whether yours would be a more effective business had your answer been Yes.

Not a difficult task — just applied common sense! If you read through the remainder of the requirements of the part of the standard which applies to your business, you will be well prepared for getting down to the task of meeting your market's needs for the 1990s.

Requirement 4.2   Quality System

This is really an overview for the setting up of a quality management system, and covers three main topics:

Requirements of the Standard

1. An outline structure is established in the form of a quality manual which summarises and references the various procedures which comprise the quality management system (QMS).

Senior management must ensure that the contents of the quality manual accurately reflect their declared policy and objectives for quality.

However, in all businesses — irrespective of size — there will be many procedures, practices, documents and records that rightly belong in the overall business administration system rather than in the quality management system. Due care should therefore be taken to identify these clearly, in order to avoid creating a bureaucratic quality system which increases operating costs without providing compensatory benefits. Further guidance on quality manuals is given in Chapter 3 and in standard ref ISO 10013.

*2. Wherever the standard uses the phrase **the supplier shall establish and maintain documented procedures for. . .** it is a mandatory requirement that actual approved practices will be accurately reflected in the documented procedures.*

BS 5750 is not a prescriptive or regulatory standard — it is purely a model of good management practice. The standard identifies only WHAT is considered to be essential for effective management. It allows each individual management team the right to decide HOW best to tackle the problem of compliance, bearing in mind the needs of their business and customers, and the available resources.

Because of this freedom to make decisions, it will be found in practice that any effective QMS is unique to the organization for which it was designed. To attempt to transpose a system designed for a large organization onto a small business will result in a totally unworkable and bureaucratic set of procedures. In the end, it will prove to be counterproductive.

Much of the adverse criticism of BS 5750 by small business management stems from a failure to appreciate that even a one-person business can meet the requirements of the standard to the satisfaction of an external assessment body, without suffering from excessive paperwork and record-keeping.

3. *Quality planning.* It was John Ruskin, the 19th Century art critic and economist, who said that "Quality is the result of intelligent effort."

This is still pertinent over a hundred years later. No business, however small, can be considered as being managed effectively unless there is clear evidence that management have focussed intelligence and effort on planning all activities relevant to the meeting of their customers' requirements. Failure to plan invariably results in the need to take often costly corrective actions at a later date, eating into profits.

Requirement 4.3   Contract Review

Many managers in small business enterprises (SMEs) fail to understand the true significance of this requirement. Before we attempt to plan how to meet the requirement, therefore, let us consider exactly what a 'contract' is. A contract is the means by which a supplier accepts an obligation to satisfy a purchaser's requirements.

The sequence of communications between the purchaser and the supplier must always include the following four written or verbal activities:

An enquiry — This is a statement of requirements originating from the purchaser, and is sometimes called an invitation to tender.

An offer — This is a response by the supplier, advising the purchaser how it is proposed to satisfy his requirements, and stating the fee or price to be charged for this service. This may be simply the identification of an existing product or service available from the supplier, or it may be a unique response detailing both technical and commercial information. It is also called the submission of a tender.

Acceptance of the offer — This is the response by the purchaser to the supplier's offer. It may be either written or verbal, and may modify the supplier's offer or the purchaser's original requirements. When in a written format, this response is often called the purchase order and should refer to both commercial and technical requirements. (This will be discussed further under Requirement 4.6.)

The acknowledgement — This is the unreserved acceptance by the supplier of his obligation fully to meet the purchaser's specified requirements in return for the agreed price or fee. This acceptance is often implied by work actually starting rather than by a formal documented acknowledgement.

A contract exists only when these four activities have been completed by the two parties concerned — the purchaser and the supplier.

Many SMEs carry out these activities in a very informal manner, which often results later in customer complaints. In order to prevent this, let us now consider how the requirements of the standard can be met in a simple but effective manner.

It is essential that a documented procedure for the review of contracts covers the following points:

- First, it should be clear WHO is responsible for reviewing all tenders and incoming contracts/purchase orders. This may be one or more nominated members of staff — it is not sufficient just to identify a department. The procedure must identify either a person, specific postholder, or group of postholders — e.g. Sales Director, or Project Manager and Works Manager. Individual limits of authority should also be clearly stated in respect of the value or type of product for which orders may be accepted without reference to a higher authority, such as the CEO or even the exectutive board.

- Secondly, decide WHAT the reviewer(s) should consider.

The standard requires that each contract is reviewed to ensure that the following points are dealt with.

a)   *The requirements must be adequately defined and documented.*

This means the reviewer(s) must be able to identify and understand exactly what a purchaser requires and expects, both technically and commercially. This should be in a suitable format to enable later reference to be made to this information whenever necessary.

b) *Any requirements differing from those in the tender must be resolved and an acceptance specification agreed.*

The reviewer(s) should always be careful to watch out for any changes which may have occurred in the technical and/or commercial information. Many purchasers identify their actual terms and conditions of purchase only in the small print of the purchase order. It is all too easy for these to be overlooked by the reviewer. Similarly, what may appear to be very minor differences between the technical and commercial information in the contract and the tender — if not identified and fully considered prior to acceptance — may lead to disputes at a later date.

c) *It should be confirmed that the supplier has the capability to meet contractual requirements.*

This means that the reviewer(s) must give due consideration to the effective use of all available resources, in order to ensure that the purchaser's requirements can be fully and promptly met. This aspect of the review should cover the allocation of available skills, equipment and stock levels in relation to other work in hand, and should also address the need for the involvement of subcontractors.

The methods by which all internal communications take place between departments and individuals within the supplier's organization should be clearly set down. There must also be a clear statement of individual responsibilities, authorities and methods to be used for seeking clarification from the purchaser of specified requirements, and/or negotiating any required changes.

After initial acceptance by the supplier, all subsequent changes to the contract should also be subject to a further review procedure prior to acceptance.

As each business is unique, so must each procedure within a business be unique, because of the executive management's freedom to make decisions regarding the most effective use of the available resources. However, in order to demonstrate compliance with ISO 9000, the supplier

Requirements of the Standard

must be able to produce not only documented procedures reflecting the above-mentioned aspects of contract review, but also records containing objective evidence of compliance. Such records, depending on the size and complexity of the business undertaken, may consist of a comprehensive file containing copies of all correspondence between purchaser and supplier, together with copies of all internal communications and minutes of internal meetings relating to each contract.

Some companies may wish to keep the records of the technical review and the commercial review completely separate for reasons of commercial confidentiality.

However, in many small businesses, a simple signature or even the initial of the authorised reviewer(s), together with the application of a suitable stamp, is all that is necessary to verify that each incoming contract has been reviewed in accordance with the relevant procedure prior to acceptance.

Where the company receives orders and inquiries by post, fax, telex or special delivery service, these will require document control. Many companies find it useful to maintain a record of receipt by the use of date stamps and/or registers. Possible entry points must be clearly identified and procedures established to ensure correct handling.

However, in many businesses, inquiries and orders will be received by phone. Due consideration must be given to who is authorised to receive them, and how they are to be suitably recorded so that subsequent actions may take place. Telephone inquiry/order pro formas or computer data files are methods in common use. Initial jottings on scraps of paper should be converted into a more durable documented format at the earliest opportunity to prevent loss or muddle.

The next item to be considered is who is authorised to review tenders and incoming orders and enquiries, and who is responsible for reviewing all inquiries and orders received by the company.

By mutual agreement, the supplier may also offer part of the contract to third parties, where their products or services are required in support of the prime contract. Such third parties are known as 'subcontractors' and their selection and control will be considered under Requirement 4.6.2.

Requirement 4.4   Design Control

No management will wish to inhibit the 'creativity' of their design staff. However, it is essential that such activities are controlled to ensure cost-effective application of resources, both human and material. No amount of careful production, inspection and testing can compensate for a poor design. Each and every design activity and its appropriate level of resources, therefore, needs to be identified. The creation of a *quality plan* for each design project is an essential part of effective management.

There is nothing new about this approach. Even the acknowledged masters of the past built upon their intuition through effective planning.

Two key requirements to note are:

4.4.6   Design reviews — As an absolute minimum at least one formal documented design review should take place prior to initial release of a project's design output information for manufacture or implementation.

In the case of large or complex projects it is advisable to hold such design reviews at all key stages as identified in the overall design project plan.

4.4.8   Design validation — Unlike design verification, which is the reconciliation of the design output documentation and data with the design input documentation and data, design validation can be carried out only on representative examples of the product or sub-modules as appropriate.

Validation is intended to demonstrate that the product will satisfy the customer's requirements for satisfactory everyday use.

Validation could be carried out by testing under simulated conditions of service, by post-installation commissioning trials, or — in the case of service industries — by a trial marketing programme.

Requirement 4.5   Documentation and Data Control

This is the requirement which many organizations find the most difficult to meet. Usually, this is because the documentation and associated data

Requirements of the Standard

within the organization have been allowed to grow to suit immediate needs, rather than as a result of careful planning.

The following are the key steps to be taken in establishing an effective control system.

1. Identify those documents/data which are pertinent to the achievement of the organization's quality objectives, including, as applicable, those of external origin either from customers or in the public domain.

2. For each class of document/data, appoint a member of staff to be personally responsible for the following:

- the most suitable medium to be used, i.e. hard copy or electronic;

- the review and approval for completeness, contents and presentation prior to authorising issue for general use;

- the establishment of a suitable register or master list;

- the control of all changes and the updating of the register or master list to prevent the use of invalid or obsolete documents.

3. Establish a company-wide document/data distribution system which will ensure that only correct and pertinent information is readily available at the point of use. Due consideration must be given to ensuring that unauthorised copies cannot be introduced into the system, and that all invalid or obsolete documents are removed, or are readily identifiable as such.

The secret of an effective document/data control system is simplicity. The number of copies in circulation should be kept to a minimum, and distributed on a *need to know* basis wherever possible.

Requirement 4.6   Purchasing

What are the key questions in deciding on a control procedure for purchasing?

4.6.2   Evaluation of Subcontractors

- Firstly, who is to be made responsible for the selection of suppliers and subcontractors? Again, this must be a nominated postholder(s).

- Secondly, how will suppliers and subcontractors be chosen?

In many SMEs, the right to choose may well be retained by the owners of the business; in larger organizations, this responsibility may well be delegated to a member of the executive management team. In either case, consideration should be given by the executive as to whether the responsibility for purchasing products and services on behalf of the company should be allocated by product, or by value, or by a combination of both factors. Even in a very small business it is undesirable for any single individual to have the sole responsibility for the purchasing function. There must always be sufficient flexibility to ensure effective control.

The choice of suppliers and subcontractors will depend on a number of possible variables, all of which must be given due consideration:

- price, availability, market reputation and/or a previous satisfactory working relationship;

- additional criteria such as information on the company's financial status and foreseeable stability, together with information on the effectiveness of its management system;

- information obtained from such sources as a Dun and Bradstreet report;

- completion of a suitable questionnaire;

- a visit to site;

- evidence of independent assessment and, possibly, registration to an appropriate part of BS 5750.

In this latter case it is important that, wherever possible, a copy of the certificate of registration should be obtained in order to verify both the declared scope of products or services covered and current issue status. The current scope and status of the issuing body should also be checked to ensure that it covers both your own and your customer's quality requirements.

A simple list of subcontractors in current use is not sufficient to meet the requirements of the standard, and every attempt possible should be made to create a comprehensive set of records of acceptable subcontractors. This body of information should be carefully considered and due weighting given to each of the above factors in determining the acceptability of a potential supplier and subcontractor. These records should be consistently reviewed and brought up to date to build up a data base on the performance of each supplier and subcontractor.

4.6.3 Purchasing Data

Just as we always look for clear and precise requirements to be stated by our own customers, so we in turn must always ensure that our own suppliers and subcontractors receive clear and precise information from us.

We should avoid unsupported references to previous verbal discussions, or ambiguous trade names. Our purchasing procedures must clearly identify just WHO has the responsibility to review and approve all outgoing purchase orders. If necessary, these may also identify the specific authorities in respect of value or types of product.

In many larger organizations, the purchase of everyday supplies for supporting services, such as catering, cleaning and office administration, may be dealt with outside the formal quality management system procedures.

4.6.4   Verification of Purchased Product

This requirement deals with a customer's right to visit a supplier's or subcontractor's works, for the purpose of checking that contractual requirements are being met. However, in order to have the right of access to subcontractors, the customer must have made this a requirement of the contract placed upon the supplier. In turn, the supplier must ensure that this requirement is advised to the subcontractors in their own purchase orders.

The standard also points out that the supplier's duty to provide an acceptable product is in no way reduced just because of a visit by the customer's representative either to inspect or to witness tests.

Requirement 4.7   Customer-supplied Product

This is often referred to as *free issue* material or equipment, which is supplied by the customer either for building into the final product or for some specialised work to be carried out. For instance, in the case of a garage business, it would be customers' cars which were in for a service. In the case of a jeweller, it could be a necklace in for repair. For a manufacturing organization, it could be special equipment or materials which are supplied.

Where it is customary for such material to be received from customers, the standard requires that there should be procedures to cover how such material and/or equipment is handled and controlled during the whole time it is in the supplier's custody. The procedures should also make it clear who is responsible for reporting any loss or damage to the customer, and how such loss or damage is to be recorded.

Any *free issue* material and/or equipment which is found to be unfit for use must also be reported.

Requirement 4.8   Product Identification & Traceability

First, let us consider the need for product identification.

Providing that the product is tangible (unlike a service), it is readily accepted that there must be some means of checking exactly what its type, style, grade, issue or other precise identification is. This can most easily be achieved by the use of suitable markings, tags or labels, and appropriate procedures can define the method most suitable for different types of product. For example, bars or sheets of metal are often marked with a colour code to identify the specification and grade of the material, together with a unique number to facilitate traceability back to the original manufacturer's records.

Product traceability, however, is required only when a customer has made it a specific contract requirement, or when a company's own management have decided that it is necessary. This might be because it would enable them to undertake a more efficient product recall or investigation in the event of problems being discovered after delivery to customers has begun, in the case of volume production, or because information on individual batches would be of assistance to management for other reasons, such as process analysis studies.

When traceability is undertaken, it is important that the degree of traceability required is clearly identified from the start and that the necessary responsibility for the keeping of suitable records is clearly defined.

Requirement 4.9   Process Control

This will obviously differ from company to company in respect of products, equipment and methods used. The key questions for consideration by a company's management are:

- What evidence is there of a controlled approach?

- Have the methods by which the product or service is to be produced and, if necessary, installed been thought through and defined either in writing or by means of a process flow chart?

- Have the production and installation tools and equipment required been identified and made available?

- Have all personnel the necessary levels of knowledge and skills to enable them to operate the equipment and understand the process needs?

- Are specific, detailed work instructions required to supplement skills and knowledge acquired by training ?

- Can compliance to specified requirements be checked by measurement or test, and is the necessary equipment available?

- Where direct measurement or test is either impracticable or uneconomic, representative samples of acceptable standards of workmanship should be agreed between all interested parties, including, wherever practicable, the customer. This often covers such cosmetic factors as finish and/or general appearance. It is much better to get agreement from the start than to have differences of opinion arising when the product is ready for delivery and acceptance by the customer.

Due consideration must be given to the monitoring and control of all processes where satisfactory results cannot be checked completely by subsequent inspection and test on completion of the process, and where any process deficiencies may become apparent only after the product has been delivered to the customer and is in use.

Typical examples of such processes are most finishes which entail painting, coating or plating, and the sterilisation and irradiation processes now widely used in the food industries. The welding and heat treatments used in the engineering industries are also examples of processes where special precautions are necessary.

Whatever the ultimate product may be, maintenance of process equipment, training of personnel, conduct of capability tests and record-keeping should all be planned as part of the effective control of the production process. It is here, in the area of process control, that we must be extra careful that all procedures, work instructions and methods are designed to aid effective production and to prevent unscheduled costs occurring due to scrap or rework. What we must avoid is the creation of an unworkable bureaucratic constraint.

Requirement 4.10 Inspection and Testing

Most SMEs, including those in the service industries, will be familiar with the need to carry out some form of inspection and/or test of their products, including goods, materials and services received from their own suppliers or subcontractors. Such tests and checks should be clearly identified in either product/project based quality plans or procedures as previously identified under Requirement 4.2.3 (Quality Planning).

Requirement 4.11 Control of Inspection, Measuring and Test Equipment

Where a manufacturer relies on measuring or test equipment — including test software — to demonstrate conformance of a product to specified requirements, great care must be exercised in its selection, handling, storage and use. Calibration to the requirements of the standard should be demonstrated. Inaccurate or unreliable equipment will inevitably result in problems, customer complaints, and the additional costs of rectification.

This is still the case, even if your customer provides you with such equipment, or if it is obtained on loan from other sources. These may include your own staff, who may provide their own simple measuring equipment such as micrometers, verniers or even electrical measuring equipment. It is therefore not advisable to allow this.

You, as the ultimate supplier, are responsible for maintaining the effectiveness of all measuring and test equipment which can affect product quality.

Methods of control are discussed more fully in Chapter 5 of this book and in ISO 10012.

Requirement 4.12 Inspection and Test Status

In order to ensure that only products which have met the relevant specified requirements are used, installed or delivered to the customer, it is essential that their inspection status can be readily identified at all times.

There are a number of ways in which this can be achieved. The inspection status of the product can be identified by the use of stamps or markings directly on the product or associated documentation, or by the use of labels or tags attached to the product. Where practicable, status can be identified solely by physical location.

Providing it is effective, any suitable means may be used for the identification of the test or inspection status of a product.

Requirement 4.13 Control of Nonconforming Product

Even in the best of companies, nonconforming products will occur from time to time. When this happens, it is essential that effective steps are taken to prevent accidental use or delivery. This can be achieved by suitable labelling or, if practicable, segregation from products which are known to be satisfactory. Some companies will even go as far as creating a dedicated quarantine area or store for such nonconforming products.

Once they have been identified, it is necessary to decide on the most cost-effective way to deal with them. Suitable members of staff should be given the necessary authority and responsibility to enable them to decide how best to handle the situation.

The first, and most cost-effective, option is to see if they can be used as produced, even if they do not strictly meet the specified requirements. This must be discussed with either the customer or the relevant design authority who could, if in agreement, authorise a waiver or concession.

The second option may be to regrade the nonconforming product and offer it for sale at a reduced price. We are all familiar with the 'bargains' offered as seconds by some industries — better a reduction in profit than a complete loss!

Sometimes it may be possible to rework or repair the nonconforming product. In this case, it is essential that documented procedures or work instructions are established to ensure that a full re-inspection is carried out on completion.

If none of the above options is possible, the nonconforming product must be either scrapped, or rejected and returned to its original supplier.

Requirement 4.14 Corrective and Preventive Action

All managers, particularly those employed in SMEs, have to develop trouble-shooting skills. Unfortunately, few develop the wider skills required to identify the real causes of problems and hence take effective action to prevent their recurrence. This requirement to address the causes of problems, including those identified by customer complaints, may therefore be one of the greatest benefits to be gained from the use of BS 5750 as a quality system model.

Requirement 4.15 Handling, Storage, Packaging, Preservation and Delivery

This requirement is really the application of common sense. The procedures must be written to suit the company's particular product range to ensure that, at all times, no damage or deterioration can occur due to incorrect handling, storage or packaging for delivery. It makes no sense at all to add value to materials used in the manufacturing process, if this value is then lost due to lack of care.

Each stage of the manufacturing process — from initial receipt of materials and components to the final hold point ready for packaging and delivery to the customer — must be carefully analysed to identify the requirements for movement and storage of the product. A well established method is to produce a process flow chart, and at each stage to identify the possible hazards which must be considered and guarded against.

Adequate packaging — and, where applicable, preservation — is often overlooked, especially when the actual transportation is out of the direct control of the company. Close liaison is required with customers to ensure that the product reaches them in an acceptable condition.

Where overseas deliveries have to be made, it is advisable to seek the advice of packaging and transportation specialists. The local office of the Department of Trade and Industry can often advise on the requirements for overseas deliveries.

Requirement 4.16 Quality Records

Records are the objective evidence of the operation of a quality system at all its stages. They are required to be kept, therefore, to prove the effectiveness of the implemented system, and will therefore be subject to periodic scrutiny by the auditors and assessors of the company's quality system.

The company procedures should clearly identify:

- what records are required, including pertinent subcontractor records such as material certificates/final inspection and test records, as required by the contract or purchase order;

- who is responsible for their safe-keeping and ultimate disposition;

- where they are to be kept, and for how long;

- how they are to be kept in order to prevent loss, damage or deterioration, and to ensure that they are readily retrievable when required.

Management should be careful to include in the quality system records only those which are clearly pertinent to the product, the training of personnel, and the effective operation of the quality management system. All other records should be treated as business administration records, and as such are not required to be made available to external assessors. Record keeping is discussed more fully in Chapter 6 of this book.

Requirement 4.17 Internal Quality Audits

Internal audits, together with regular executive management reviews, provide the necessary information to ensure that an organization's quality policy and objectives are being met, or to enable prompt preventive action to be taken wherever necessary.

Personnel for this task should be chosen with care, and preferably given professional training in the audit techniques to be used.

Refer to *BS 7229 — Guide to Quality Audits* for further information on this subject.

It is important that this activity is seen by all concerned to be of benefit to the whole organization. It must never be allowed to become a petty, bureaucratic, internal policing activity or the inherent benefits can be irretrievably lost.

Requirement 4.18 Training

Many SMEs claim that they cannot afford to spend money on training, especially when their profit margins are under pressure. This is a very short-sighted view, as a business can only be as effective as the staff it employs.

A planned programme to identify each individual's training needs should therefore be regarded as essential, if unscheduled costs caused by incorrect work or decisions are to be avoided. Such a programme does not have to be complex and expensive. It is sufficient if each level of supervision and management identifies exactly:

- what tasks are undertaken in their specific area of responsibility;

- what equipment is in use;

- who has the necessary knowledge and skills to operate equipment and carry out the assigned tasks.

A simple matrix or list may be all that is needed to identify each department's training requirements.

In many cases, on-the-job training against departmental procedures will be sufficient to ensure adequate cover against foreseeable occurrences, such as sickness, leave, or increased workloads. A simple record of training standards achieved should be maintained by departmental heads. Where special knowledge is required, local TECs should be able to advise on the most suitable local training source.

Requirement 4.19 Servicing

This requirement covers those activities which a supplier agrees to carry out on his product after delivery has been accepted by the customer, in addition to any corrective action which may be required under a guarantee or warranty claim. Depending on the nature of the product, servicing may be carried out at the customer's premises or by the return of the product to the supplier.

Servicing may be specified either in the original contract or in a separate contract, as required. In all cases, it is essential that the continuing effectiveness of the quality management system can be demonstrated by the existence of procedures and work instructions, as well as the training and skill of all personnel engaged in such tasks.

The usual weak areas which should be addressed are:

- control of special purpose tools and equipment;

- control of measuring and test equipment in use in the field;

- control of maintenance manuals and associated instructions;

- control of replacement parts and the disposal of failed or nonconforming parts and equipment;

- availability of technical advice for personnel working at customers' sites;

- on-going training to update field personnel with the company's latest products;

- effective feedback of service problems to design and production personnel at base.

Requirement 4.20 Statistical Techniques

Statistical techniques for the determination of acceptable quality levels in inspection plans, and for process control and capability studies, should be chosen with care from the methods listed in reference documents such as BS 600, BS 6000 and ISO Standards Handbook 3.

Consideration should also be given to the use of statistical techniques for the analysis of such activities as sales marketing, customer complaints, nonconformance, and overall quality performance data.

Chapter 3

QUALITY MANUALS & PROCEDURES

QUALITY MANAGEMENT has been defined as:

"That aspect of the overall management function that determines and implements the quality policy"   *ISO 8402/BS 4778*

Quality assurance has been defined as:

"All those planned and systematic actions necessary to provide adequate confidence that a product or service will satisfy given requirements for quality"   *ISO 8402/BS 4778*

Therefore, if an organization's objective is to be seen as having established an effective 'quality management system' to provide 'assurance' to its customers, then it must first address the question of how all the various 'planned and systematic actions' are to be communicated effectively to all levels of its staff.

This question can best be answered by the establishment of a documented quality system based on an internationally recognised standard such as *BS 5750:1994/ISO 9000:1994*. The quality system should consist of a comprehensive set of documented departmental procedures and work instructions which provide guidance and direction to personnel at all levels throughout the organization. These are the means of defining the work to be done and of delegating necessary responsibilities and authorities to individual members of staff.

This documented system, once established, will aid everyone's understanding of management's requirements. It will ensure uniformity of performance when the inevitable changes in personnel occur. Formal procedures are an aid to training, enabling new staff to be introduced quickly to the organization's established working practices. The system will also serve as reference criteria for management and customers alike when assessing the effectiveness of the organization's assurance of quality. Most managers readily accept that, without some system of formalised procedures, the probability of variations in individual performance in meeting customers' requirements is increased in proportion to the complexity of the organization.

However, an uncontrolled bureaucracy will create more problems than it solves. The secret of any effective system is simplicity; this must constantly be borne in mind during the development of the quality manual and associated departmental procedures.

What is a "quality manual" ?

It is a convenient method by which an organization's general quality policy, procedures and practices can be brought to the attention of its employees.

It can also be used to demonstrate to potential purchasers that the organization is capable of meeting the requirements of internationally recognised quality system standards such as BS 5750/ISO 9000.

What benefits are there in producing a quality manual?

Apart from providing a concise means of conveying information to employees and potential customers, the quality manual may also offer the following benefits.

Product Liability

The existence of a documented set of authorised procedures and work instructions in the form of a quality manual will readily demonstrate that management have taken reasonable measures to ensure that goods are safe and fit for their intended purpose.

Management Audit and Review

The quality manual provides the management team with the necessary criteria for monitoring the effective implementation of the organization's quality policy, enabling them to take corrective action where necessary to reduce rework or scrap. This leads to increased profitability and competitiveness.

External Assessments & Audits

The quality manual will be used by customers' representatives and/or assessors working for one of the national certification bodies in verifying the organization's state of compliance with BS 5750.

Who should write the quality manual?

A quality manual is only a means to an end: the effective communication of the organization's management requirements to ensure that its customers' needs are met. Hence the actual writing of the manual must be seen as a collective management task to which all possible levels of staff have contributed. Product quality is ensured by competent and motivated people, not just pieces of paper. The prime task is therefore to ensure that the quality manual is a true reflection of the organization's quality policy and working practices.

Each quality manual must be unique to the organization whose QMS it describes. Trying to adapt another company's or consultant's manual and procedures to your own use to save time and money will not be effective in the long term. At best, it may result in the application of a bureaucratic and unsuitable system, and at worst it may create a system which no one really owns and which is effectively ignored.

However, whilst departmental involvement is vital to generate a sense of ownership in the resulting procedures and work instructions, a co-ordinator is essential to ensure continuity and coherence and to avoid gaps and duplication in the prescribed quality system. A possible choice for the co-ordinator would be the 'management representative' who, in the words of BS 5750, "...shall have defined responsibility and authority for ensuring that a quality system is established, implemented and maintained in accordance with this International Standard".

Ultimately, the quality manual should be issued under the approval of the chief executive as a clear statement of the management's requirements.

What should the quality manual contain?

Whilst the detailed contents of individual quality manuals will depend on the size, nature and complexity of the organization, certain elements are common to all manuals:

Foreword

This is usually a brief statement of the manual's purpose, over the signature of the organization's management representative.

Distribution Control

This should identify the holders of all copies of the manual, including, as appropriate, certification bodies and key customers whose copies will be subject to amendment or reissue.

To avoid unnecessary complications in the upkeep of manuals, the list of controlled copy-holders should be kept as short as possible, and departmental heads made responsible for ensuring that all their staff fully understand and implement the relevant procedures.

Copies of the manual may also be made available to potential customers and other interested parties. However, as these will not be the subject of periodic updating, they must be stamped or otherwise identified as an 'uncontrolled copy' prior to issue.

Amendments & Reissue

All controlled copies of the manual must be updated in accordance with the organization's procedure for document change control.

It is essential that responsibilities for the upkeep of individual manuals are clearly defined and that obsolete pages are promptly removed and destroyed from all controlled copies.

Terms & Definitions

All industries and even some individual organizations develop their own terminology or jargon. To prevent any possible misunderstandings, it is advisable to list and define the meaning of any special terms used in the quality manual.

Policy Statement

ISO 8402/BS 4778 — Quality Vocabulary International Terms defines quality policy as the *"overall quality intentions and direction of an organization as regards quality, as formally expressed by top management"*.

BS 5750 states that *"The supplier's management with executive responsibility shall define and document its policy for quality, including objectives for quality and its commitment to quality. The quality policy shall be relevant to the supplier's organizational goals and the expectations and needs of its customers."*

The quality policy must therefore be seen to be an integral part of the organization's overall business policy. There must be objective evidence available that the quality policy is "understood, implemented and maintained at all levels in the organization". Thus there should be a clear and precise written statement by the chief executive of the organization's policy and objectives for, and commitment to, product quality.

Such a statement might go beyond just meeting the strict requirements of BS 5750. It could usefully include top management's recognition of the importance of the 'internal customer' in meeting the organization's own internal requirements throughout all aspects of its operations and interdepartmental interfaces.

Because quality is a concept, top management must make their own interpretation of what quality means in relation to both the needs of the organization and the expectations of their customers in respect of the organization's products and services. Policy statements such as "we are committed to quality", without any explanation of how and why, should be avoided at all costs. Instead, the quality policy should be a simple and easily understood statement of management commitments and targets, supported by clearly-defined objectives which are capable of achievement by all personnel.

Consideration should be given to including the following in the quality policy statement:

- what quality means to the organization;

- why quality is important to the organization;

- who is responsible for quality within the organization;

- the quality objectives of the organization.

Quality objectives should always be aimed at improving the organization's ability to survive in an increasingly competitive market, not only by meeting customer requirements but also by exceeding their expectations at an acceptable cost.

The task of drafting the quality policy and setting feasible objectives is one to which people at every level of an organization can contribute; only in this way can the understanding and commitment of all concerned be guaranteed.

Quality Policy Implementation

Whilst quality can be said to be everybody's responsibility, it is essential that a representative of the management team be appointed to act as a focal point to ensure that the organization's quality policy is implemented effectively.

Quality Manuals & Procedures

Company Organization

This section of the manual can be used to give a brief outline of the scope of the organization's products and background, and to identify the overall management structure.

Whilst charts may be useful for indicating the organization's general reporting structure, more detailed information will be required to define the actual responsibilities and authorities of individual post-holders.

Company Quality Assurance System

Although for ease of subsequent review it is preferable to follow the format of BS 5750, this may not always be possible or desirable when procedures already exist which have proved satisfactory in meeting the needs of the organization and its customers. In such cases, the management representative should always remember that the primary purpose of a quality manual is to provide an adequate description of the company's quality system, while serving as a permanent reference for the implementation and maintenance of that system by company personnel. The quality manual should never be produced solely for the convenience of auditors or external assessors.

While a very small organization may include all its procedures and work instructions within one quality manual, many organizations prefer to create a three, or even four, tier system for ease of control and distribution.

BS 5750 states that the organization's management *"shall establish and maintain a documented system as a means of ensuring that product conforms to specified requirements"*. This requires that, wherever the standard uses the phrase *"the supplier shall establish and maintain procedures for . . ."*, the relevant activity must be seen to be controlled by a written procedure which states simply and clearly the following:

Scope
This refers to what the activity comprises, and the quality objectives.

Responsibilities
This shows who has been delegated the necessary authority and responsibility to attain the assigned quality objectives.

Method
This refers to how the designated level of management or supervision has determined that the assigned quality objectives can be met with maximum efficiency and, where applicable, lists the criteria to be satisfied.

Procedures usually refer to departmental or interdepartmental methods of operation and thus remain relatively constant, regardless of the product or service. Their purpose is to act as a reference of acceptable practice to all personnel, including new appointees. They are also the means by which management can audit and review current practice, and initiate any necessary changes to achieve their objectives.

It is, however, people who produce a product or service - not pieces of paper. Procedures must therefore never be allowed to become a constraint on the prime objectives of the organization, which are to meet or exceed customers' expectations in the most economical way. Procedures must always be sufficiently flexible to meet foreseeable operational needs, such as assigned personnel being off site due to sickness, leave or alternative duties.

The documented system should never be looked upon as something to be bypassed when under pressure. In fact, it is under these circumstances that the documented procedures are most needed, to ensure that the declared quality objectives are met. Procedures, therefore, should always clearly identify who has the authority to take decisions if an abnormal situation occurs.

BS 5750 also makes reference to the need for documented procedures in respect of activities such as production, installation and servicing, where the absence of such procedures could adversely affect quality. Such procedures are generally product specific and are required as a reference source to supplement basic skills and knowledge acquired by training.

Many SMEs will already have established adequate 'work instructions' for their manufacturing processes, and where this is the case no further action will be necessary, other than to ensure such work instructions are covered by their documentation control system.

A procedure or work instruction should describe in sufficient detail the equipment to be used, tests to be carried out, criteria for acceptance and, where applicable, records to be kept:

- what is to be done;
- when it is to be done;
- who should do it;
- how it should be done.

Wherever possible, procedures and work instructions should reference associated documents, including pro formas and labels to be used by personnel carrying out the assigned task. All documented procedures and work instructions must be reviewed and approved for adequacy by authorised personnel prior to general issue, and be subject to the organization's document control procedures, particularly in respect of any subsequent changes. It is good practice for all procedures and work instructions to have a unique reference number and issue number, and to be signed by the approving authority. BS 5750 also requires, for the purposes of effective document control, that a master list of procedures and work instructions is established and then kept up to date, to enable the ready identification of the current revision status of all quality system documents.

In many organizations, system and process flow charts or algorithms may be the best method of effective communication: think how much information is available from London Transport's graphic depicting the London underground rail system.

A typical list of procedures required to comply with the requirements of BS 5750: Part 1 / ISO 9001 is set out on the following page. Additional procedures may be required at the discretion of a company's management to ensure that its products conform to specific requirements. The company's quality control policy and objectives may also be made available to all personnel — in addition to its inclusion in the quality manual — by means of a memo from the CEO or via notice boards.

PROCEDURES

ACTIVITY	BS. Ref.	REMARKS
Contract Review	4.3	Note need for records
Design Control	4.4	Management of the design process
	4.4.9	Management of design changes
Document Control	4.5	Including computerised data and externally supplied documents
Purchasing	4.6	Selection of subcontractors and control of purchasing data
Control of Customer-supplied Product	4.7	Free issue material, components or equipment — note need for records
Product Identification and Traceability	4.8	Note need for records if traceability is a specified requirement
Process Control	4.9	When its absence could adversely affect product quality
Inspection & Testing	4.10	A contract / product based quality plan may be used in lieu
Inspection, Measuring & Test Equipment	4.11	Control and calibration
Control of Nonconforming Product	4.13	Identification, and product-holding pending disposition
Corrective and Preventive Action	4.14	Investigation of problems, analysis and planning for future prevention
Handling, Storage, Packaging, Preservation and Delivery	4.15	Where required by contract, delivery to the customer's nominated site may be the supplier's responsibility
Quality Records	4.16	What, Where, Who and How they are maintained
Internal Quality Audits	4.17	What, Where, Who and How they are carried out
Training	4.18	Identification of needs and keeping of records
Servicing	4.19	Only required where servicing is specified in a contract
Statistical Techniques	4.20	Only required when statistical techniques are used for establishing, controlling and verifying process capability and product characteristics

QUALITY SYSTEM DOCUMENTATION

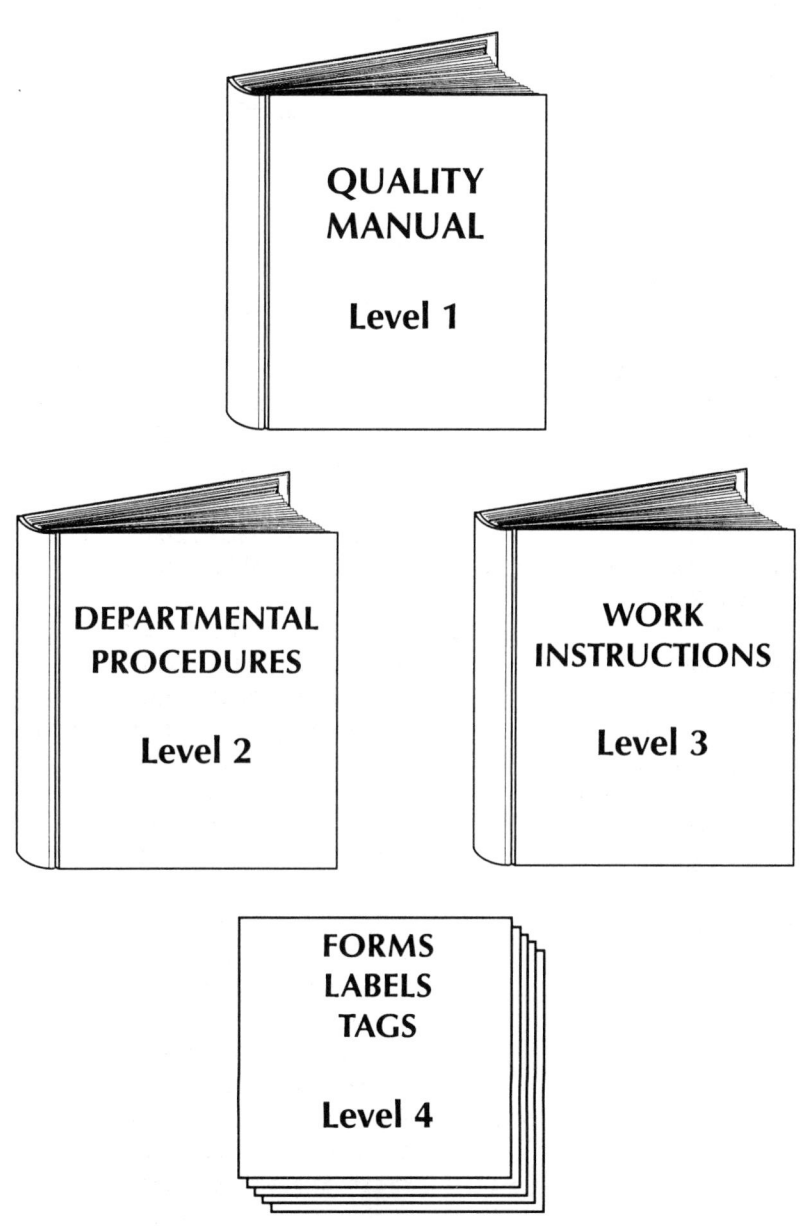

Example of Level 2 Documentation

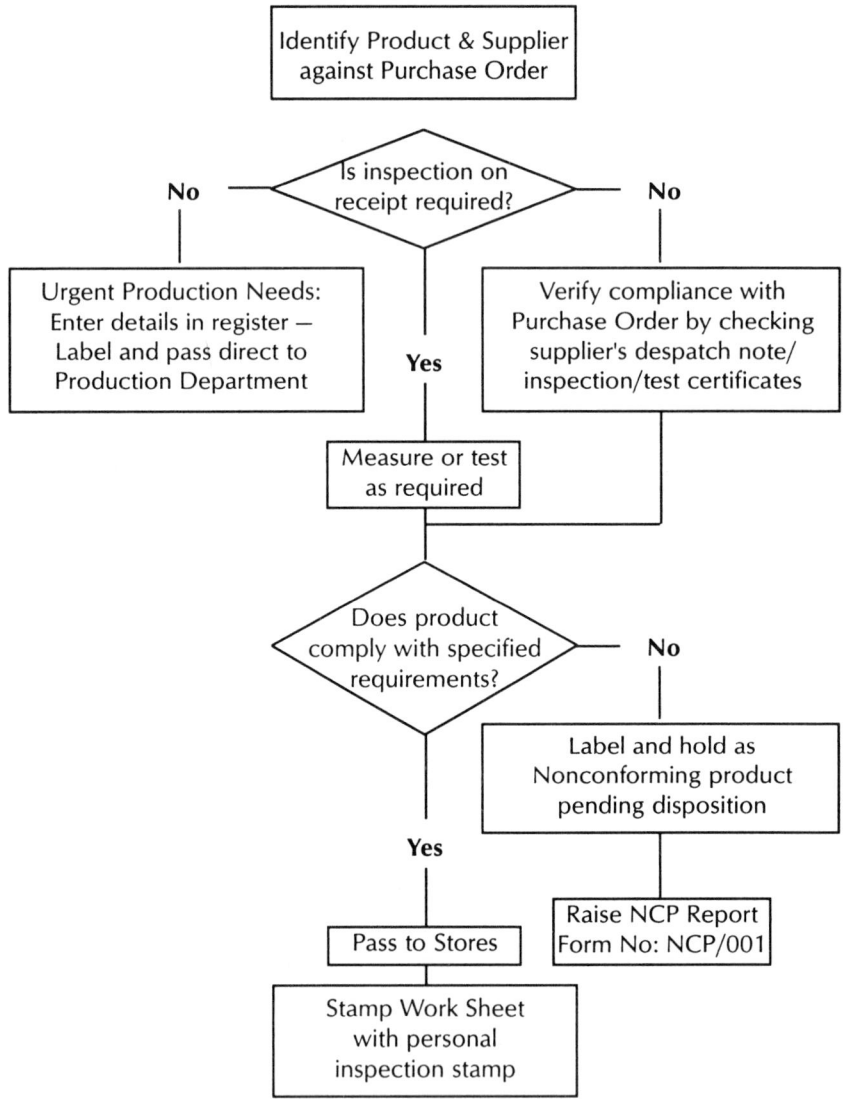

Goods Receiving Flow Sheet

Example of Level 3 Documentation

```
                    Start
                      │
              ┌───────▼───────┐
              │ Switch on power│
              └───────┬───────┘
              ┌───────▼───────┐
              │Power on self test│
              └───────┬───────┘
                      │
      No      ◄────── Error ──────►     Yes
       │                                 │
┌──────▼──────┐                  ┌───────▼───────┐
│Set up component│                │ Error message │
│   for test    │                │   displayed   │
└──────┬──────┘                  └───────┬───────┘
       │                                 │
┌──────▼──────┐                  ┌───────▼───────┐
│Enter component│                 │Turn off test set│
│ part number  │                  └───────┬───────┘
└──────┬──────┘                          │
┌──────▼──────┐                  ┌───────▼───────┐
│   Run test   │                  │Notify supervisor│
└──────┬──────┘                  └───────────────┘
       │
     Test
    result  ──────►  No
 satisfactory
       │
      Yes                    ┌──────────────────┐
┌──────▼──────┐              │ Label and hold as │
│Attach Passed │ ◄──────►    │Nonconforming product│
│Inspection label│            │pending disposition │
└──────┬──────┘              └─────────┬────────┘
       │                               │
       └──────┤Select next component for test│
```

Typical Test Instruction for Automatic Test Equipment

Example of Level 4 Documentation

Typical Goods Received Inspection Stamps or Labels

Chapter 4

IMPLEMENTING THE DOCUMENTED QUALITY SYSTEM

ALL BUSINESSES, however small, must have procedures and practices in order to function on a day-to-day basis. However, in most cases, these have been established by trial and error and now form part of the routine custom and practice of the people currently employed by the business. Whilst they may be considered satisfactory by the individuals concerned, it is impossible to use such methods for training new staff, or indeed for management audits. A change of staff will invariably result in a change of practice and hence an unacceptable level of variability could be introduced.

In order to comply with the requirements of BS 5750, the established day-to-day practices must be converted into documented procedures which may serve as the basis for the training of new staff and for internal audits, and act as a source of reference for existing staff. The standard identifies where procedures are a requirement by the use of the phrase *"the supplier shall establish and maintain documented procedures for...."*

Unfortunately, most people in small businesses are not used to formal procedures. They feel that these serve no useful purpose, as they already know how to do their jobs. There is also a "hidden reason" for avoiding formal procedures, particularly on the part of supervisors and managers, who fear that documenting their working practices will mean that their hard-earned "expertise" will now be readily available to all their colleagues, which could harm their future promotion or even prospects of employment. We all like to feel that we are indispensable.

To overcome these preconceptions requires considerable powers of leadership and diplomacy on the part of senior management and their appointed management representative. Any attempt to 'impose' a documented quality system must be avoided at all costs, and therefore the use of external consultants in the early stages may prove counterproductive for the small business. It would be more effective for the CEO to:

- explain to all staff exactly why the company has decided to establish a quality management system to meet the requirements of BS 5750;

- make a clear statement of the company's quality policy and future objectives;

- answer any questions arising, giving the necessary assurances in respect of future prospects that the staff will expect to hear;

- ask for the active co-operation of all concerned in assisting the appointed quality management representative to establish the quality management system.

Only when this mutual co-operation has been sought and given should the management representative start to identify all the activities within the organization which can rightly be considered to lie within the boundary of the quality management system. Time must be spent with each member of staff in turn to seek their assistance in establishing exactly how the business really operates. The use of flow charts is a very effective method of reaching mutual understanding. For many small businesses the use of such flow charts, together with a minimum of the 'narrative' type of procedures and work instructions, may be all that is really needed to ensure compliance with BS 5750. *See examples given at the end of Chapter 3.*

Only when the management representative has obtained this information, and a degree of acceptance throughout the organization, should any attempt be made to relate it to BS 5750. Even at this stage,

Implementing The Documented Quality System

the prime documents in the BS 5750/ISO 9000 series to be studied are NOT Parts 1,2 or 3/ISO 9001,9002,9003, but the guidelines: BS 5750 Part 0:Section 0.2/ISO 9004 for manufacturing organizations; BS 5750 Part 8/ISO 9004-2 for service organizations; and BS 5750 Part 13/ISO 9000-3 for software organizations.

Only when these documents have been studied and completely understood will the management representative be in a position to finalise the documented quality system to meet the requirements of BS 5750 Part 1, 2 or 3 (whichever is appropriate to the type of products or service offered by the organization to its customers).

Now is the moment when senior management and their representative should consider either seeking further training or employing external consultants. Whatever their decision, the resultant QMS must remain firmly the company's own unique system for, without this sense of ownership, it is unlikely that employees will be willing to commit themselves to continuing compliance.

Once the documented system has been agreed, authorised and issued for use, the management representative should start setting up the internal audit and management review programme. Initially, some fine tuning will inevitably be required and, here again, it is essential that all concerned give their active co-operation. (Chapter 7 gives more information on internal audits and management reviews.)

After at least six months of active implementation, once the senior management are satisfied with the stability of the QMS, consideration can be given to seeking external assessment and registration.

The number of organizations accredited by the President of the Board of Trade as being competent to make independent assessments of quality management systems against the requirements of BS 5750, and to issue certificates of registration, continues to increase. Perhaps on the principle that so-called free market forces will ultimately control the cost of registration, the National Accreditation Council of Certification Bodies (NACCB) listed no fewer than 36 accredited certification bodies at June 1994, with several more under consideration.

While this may give small businesses the opportunity to shop around for the best available deal, the cheapest certification package may not prove to be the most cost-effective in the long term. It is advisable to seek information on the actual scope of a certification body's accreditation against the Standard Industrial Classification (SIC) codes, and on the extent of recognition of its certification by the company's customers in Europe and in the wider international market. It is probably best to obtain at least three separate quotations and to compare the costs of assessment and registration over a three-year period, rather than simply to compare the initial cost. Failure to take these precautions may result in the expenditure of a great deal of time, effort and money, only to end up with a virtually useless certificate of registration. (Chapter 8 gives further information on the selection of a certification body.)

Some of our broadsheet newspapers have recently published articles which criticise the apparently uncontrolled proliferation of organizations offering consultancy and certification services in the UK, and challenge the need for small businesses to be registered to BS 5750. To make their point, many of the articles have been deliberately biased against BS 5750, omitting also to mention the wider acceptance of the ISO 9000 equivalent standards by the international business community.

These articles have, however, performed a useful service in identifying how many larger organizations, both in the public and private sectors, are pursuing a policy of purchasing goods and services only from BS 5750 registered companies, without giving due thought to the possible heavy costs this policy will impose on their supplier base. These are costs which the market will have to bear when many of the smaller firms, which have been meeting their needs for years, are driven out of business by such unthinking demands.

For many of these small businesses, while BS 5750 undoubtedly has much to offer as a model for effective management, strict compliance as demanded by the certification bodies may well place a bureaucratic constraint on the cost-effective day-to-day management of the business, as well as imposing an additional burden on already over-committed resources.

How can small businesses tackle this problem? Only by fully discussing the anticipated cost/benefits with their customers at the highest possible level, bearing in mind that BS 5750 does not itself demand that suppliers and subcontractors seek independent third-party registration. The standard requires only that records of acceptable subcontractors are established and maintained. The criteria for acceptability must always be determined between supplier and purchaser and can be based upon previously demonstrated capability and performance.

Once the decision has been taken to seek external assessment and registration, and the certification body chosen, what is now required of the organization's management?

Planning for a successful assessment

The formal notification of forthcoming assessment will be addressed to the company's chief executive by the assessment team leader. The CEO should appoint an assessment co-ordinator who has full responsibility for the co-ordination of all company activities relevant to the forthcoming assessment — normally the management representative.

Analysis shows that 80% of firms assessed initially fail to meet the requirements set out in the standard. A major reason for this is their lack of effective preassessment planning.

An assessment should be regarded by senior management as a unique opportunity to SELL the company — its management as well as its products — to an important client, as represented by the assessment team. The assessment co-ordinator has the task of stage-managing this sales promotion.

The following guidelines have been proven in practice as significantly increasing a company's chances of 'first time' success.

PART 1. Preassessment Activities

   1. On appointment, the assessment co-ordinator should check to ensure that the quality manual and associated quality control documentation are fully up to date and accurately reflect both the requirements of the standard and current company practice. Until this has been achieved the assessment should not be proceeded with.

   2. The declared "scope of company products and services" should be checked for accuracy against current practice.

3. The company's current internal audit and review programme should be checked, paying particular attention to any outstanding audits and/or corrective actions. If for any reason these cannot be completed prior to the proposed date of assessment, then it is essential that the company's position should be explained to the assessment team leader, who may decide to defer assessment to a later date.

4. A copy of the company's quality manual and scope of work should be sent to the appointed assessment team leader under cover of a letter from the CEO formally inviting the assessment team to visit and notifying the appointment of the company's assessment co-ordinator.

5. The assessment team leader and assessment co-ordinator should now liaise. If thought necessary, a preassessment visit should be arranged, to establish the following:

- number and required expertise of assessment team;
- mutually acceptable dates — normally 2 to 5 days, depending on the size and/or complexity of firm;
- hotel, local transport, meal arrangements;
- use of company facilities — office, typing, copying, phones;
- a provisional programme for the assessment;
- availability of senior management.

6. Following this preassessment discussion, the assessment team leader will formally advise the company of the agreed programme.

7. On receipt of this, the CEO should circulate the programme to all senior line management, requesting them to be available as required by the programme. They should be reminded that the assessment must be looked upon as a 'sales opportunity' and the assessors not as 'opponents'.

Implementing The Documented Quality System

Nothing must be given higher priority on the day than fully satisfying the needs of the assessment team.

Effective quality management is more than compliance with paperwork procedures and specifications. It is an attitude of mind. It is not only the management of quality which will be assessed, but also the quality of management. A highly visible commitment by senior management is crucial to the achievement of a successful assessment.

8. Company staff/union representatives should also be fully briefed on the assessment programme to prevent any adverse industrial relations developing.

9. The assessment co-ordinator should personally brief all line managers and supervisors on the role they and their departments will have to play during the assessment.

It is preferable to do this department by department, rather than collectively, and the opportunity must also be taken to brief individual employees. By the completion of this phase, everyone from the CEO downwards should have been fully briefed on the why, when and where of the forthcoming assessment, and be actively engaged in ensuring that their departments fully comply with the relevant company procedures. Creating a commitment of 'hearts and minds' is a vital part of the assessment co-ordinator's task.

PART 2. Choice of Guides

During the course of the assessment, the assessment team will require members of staff to accompany them, not only to guide them round the site but also to explain the actual working of departmental procedures and processes.

There are two approaches to this:

a) Each member of the assessment team may be allocated an individual member of staff as a guide. In this case, it is essential that such guides are fully conversant with company procedures and processes within the areas visited.

b) Either the line manager or his nominated representative may act as a guide within each department of the company to be visited by the assessment team. In this case, 'site guides' will merely be required to escort team members from their base to the point of assessment, and to make the necessary introductions to the manager and departmental guides.

In either case, the assessment co-ordinator must ensure that the chosen guides are fully briefed on their duties. Prior to the actual assessment all guides should either carry out an audit, or accompany a trained auditor, in their respective areas of responsibility. It is recommended that the assessment co-ordinator personally visits every department within two days immediately prior to the assessment and walks round with the appointed guide.

Remember that assessors require 'objective evidence' before they can record a noncompliance. Leave nothing to chance. Make sure that all work in progress is visibly under control in accordance with current company procedures.

PART 3. The Assessment

For the duration of the assessment, the assessment co-ordinator should delegate all his line management tasks to his deputy so that he can concentrate fully on the smooth running of the task in hand — the assessment.

Immediately after the initial introductions of the 'arrival meeting', the assessment co-ordinator should escort the team to their appointed base and introduce them to their respective guides.

Once the assessment is under way, the assessment co-ordinator must ensure that guides and line management alert him to any potential problems, so that he can take speedy preventive or corrective action as required.

It is advisable for the assessment co-ordinator and assessment team leader to have a final session each evening to discuss and agree any noncompliances which have arisen during the day. Here the assessment co-ordinator should be firm but fair. Above all, he must be diplomatic. It is the assessment team leader's job to ensure that all noncompliances are recorded, and equally the assessment co-ordinator's job to minimise their possible effect on the overall recommendation.

Let the words of the standard work for you, but do not argue pointlessly or attempt to defend the indefensible. Remember you are not adversaries, but professionals with a common goal — an effective quality control system.

Senior management should be fully briefed on the daily outcome and, if necessary, realistic timing for effective corrective actions should be agreed before the final meeting. This meeting should be brief, factual and professional.

PART 4. Post-Assessment

Even though the assessment has been completed and the team have departed, the assessment co-ordinator still has work to do. This will depend on the team's recommendations to their own management, which could be:

1. No noncompliances recorded or only minor noncompliances — for which the team leader is confident the company will complete the proposed corrective actions prior to the first surveillance visit — and therefore registration will be recommended.

Congratulations all round: but do tactfully suggest that the CEO personally announces the result and thanks all concerned — it was a team effort.

2. Either a major noncompliance or a significant number of minor noncompliances recorded, which the company agrees to rectify within an agreed period — up to three months maximum. The team leader decides to recommend that registration is deferred, pending verification of the corrective actions taken.

Not as good as planned — but this still calls for credit where due from the CEO.

The assessment co-ordinator must closely monitor the agreed corrective actions until objective evidence of completion can be submitted to the team leader or his nominee.

3. A significant number of major noncompliances recorded. The team leader is unable to recommend registration and considers that a complete reassessment visit will be necessary at some later date.

Where did you go wrong?

More information on assessments and the duties of guides is available in Chapters 8 and 9.

Chapter 5

CONTROL OF MEASURING AND TEST EQUIPMENT

WHILST IT is unlikely that SMEs in the service industry will need to use measuring or test equipment to check that their product meets their customers' specified requirements, all manufacturing organizations will most certainly need to use such equipment. Unless effective control of all types of measuring and test equipment can be established, there is always the risk that an unsatisfactory product will be delivered to a customer.

It is most important, therefore, that inspection and test equipment is selected very carefully to ensure that it is both suitable and fit for purpose. This means that it must be capable of being used with ease and confidence. It would be inappropriate, for instance, to try to use a steel tape to check measurements requiring a tolerance of only one micron for acceptability. However, it would be perfectly acceptable to use it for measurements with a permitted tolerance of, say, 5 mm.

Records should be kept of all measuring and test equipment available, including any loaned out to subcontractors or borrowed from customers or others, especially equipment which may be the personal property of employees. All such equipment should be subject to regular checks to ensure continuing fitness for use. The quality manual should state the calibration intervals.

Where inaccuracies in equipment could have an adverse effect on the acceptability of the product, it is essential that any differences between indicated readings and true readings are established. They may then be allowed for, or corrected where practicable, or the equipment may have to be replaced.

In order to carry out this calibration process it is necessary to use what are called 'secondary standards' which have a known relationship with the definitive physical standards kept at the National Physical Laboratory (NPL) at Teddington, or similar Government establishments. Such standards are themselves subject to regular calibration checks at special laboratories or test houses, which in turn have been approved by a Government Agency such as The National Accreditation & Measuring Service (NAMAS).

It may not always be possible to identify a nationally recognised standard, however; a good example of this is flow measurements for the calibration of domestic gas meters. In such cases, calculations or a comparison with a similar instrument may be used as the basis for calibration.

For a calibration to be effective, checks must be taken over the full range of the instrument, and all differences between indicated readings and the nominal value, as represented by the secondary standard, must be recorded to enable the continuing fitness for use to be determined. Where results of a calibration are found to be unsatisfactory, suitable corrective action must be taken. This may be both on the instrument itself and (after due consideration of the continuing acceptability of previous inspection and test results) on products previously thought to be satisfactory. If necessary, these products may require reinspection or test prior to further work or use.

Some of the more frequent questions raised about the control of measuring and test equipment are as follows:

Q. Must all measuring and test equipment be calibrated?

A. It is essential that all equipment used for the purpose of verifying that a product conforms to specified requirements is in a known and acceptable state of calibration, i.e. inspection and process control equipment.

However, regular calibration checks can be expensive. Management must therefore decide to what extent other equipment, used only as an aid to production, also needs to be calibrated, or whether regular serviceability or fitness-for-purpose checks are all that is required.

Many instruments are used purely for indication rather than for the reading of precise values. Take a clock or watch, for instance: most people would be able tell the time accurately enough for their everyday needs just by looking at the position of the hands, even if no numbers were visible. However, if the same watch or clock were used to time a process activity accurately against a critical specified requirement, then the hours, minutes and seconds would need to be readable and the calibration status known.

Q. How often should calibrations be carried out? BS 5750 only refers to "prescribed intervals".

A. The need for recalibration will depend entirely on the features of the instrument which can contribute to a change of accuracy.

In general, change will be due to wear, which in turn depends on use and care in handling. In such cases, instruments in daily use would obviously require more frequent calibration than the same type of instrument which is used only occasionally.

Other types of instrument may contain components which can deteriorate with time, irrespective of the amount of use the instrument receives. In these cases, the frequency of calibration should be determined on a 'calendar' rather than a usage basis.

By keeping comprehensive records of actual indicated readings whenever a calibration is carried out, any trend for an instrument to drift outside acceptable limits can be observed and the frequency of calibration adjusted accordingly.

Ideally, recalibration should be carried out only 'just in time' to prevent the instrument becoming unfit for further use. However, in practice, it may be more cost-effective to arrange for batches of instruments to be recalibrated against a predetermined programme scheduled to meet operational needs. In this case, the frequency of calibration must take into account all the factors affecting change. Plan for the worst case, initially; then gradually extend the time between calibrations as experience dictates.

Although advice from the original manufacturers of an instrument and from specialised test laboratories is invaluable, the final decision rests with a company's own management.

Q. Must calibration be carried out only in a temperature-controlled environment?

A. No. Although such environmental factors as temperature, pressure and humidity may have an effect on the readings obtained, a controlled environment is essential only for the calibration of specialised instruments capable of great accuracy and precision.

Normally, a common-sense approach to ensure that there are no significant temperature differences between the instrument, the referent standard and the general surroundings is all that is required. If in doubt, it is advisable to let the instrument and the standard stabilise for a few hours before calibration is carried out.

Q. What do "measurement uncertainty", "accuracy" and "precision" mean in practical terms?

A.

Measurement uncertainty:

There are many factors that may affect the true value of a measurement and the indicated reading of the instrument used. These include: the number of secondary standards in the traceability trail between the actual referent standard used in the calibration of the instrument and the national physical standard held at the NPL or equivalent international laboratory; the interface between the measuring equipment and the person using it; and the environmental conditions in which it is being used, which may include such variables as temperature, pressure, humidity, vibration, cleanliness, electromagnetic interference, and lighting.

The effect on the true value of a measurement can be estimated using statistical data and correction factors to give a estimated range

CONTROL OF MEASURING AND TEST EQUIPMENT

within which the true value will lie.

Calibration certificates issued by a NAMAS-approved laboratory should clearly state the estimated "uncertainty of measurement", and this should be taken into account when selecting measuring and test equipment and referent standards for a particular task in relation to the product acceptance limits.

Accuracy:

This is the closeness between the indicated reading of the instrument and the estimated true value of the measurement.

A good rule of thumb is to choose a measuring instrument which is capable of an accuracy at least ten times greater than the permissible specified acceptable product tolerances.

Precision:

This term is often incorrectly used when "accuracy" is really intended. "Precision", as used in metrology, refers to the closeness of agreement between repeated measurements in a stable environment, and depends on the 'robustness' of the instrument and the interface with the user.

Q. Must all measuring and test equipment have a calibration label fixed to it?

A. No. Whilst a secure self-adhesive or tie-on label is possibly the most direct method of giving information on an instrument's use, such as the date when the next recalibration is due, this may not be practicable under everyday conditions of use.

In such cases, it may be better to mark the actual instrument with a suitable identity number, and a colour or reference code, which will both indicate its current calibration status and enable reference to be made to the instrument's records for further information.

Multi-range instruments may have limitations of use on some of the ranges available. This should always be clearly marked on the instrument to avoid incorrect use.

Equipment which has been classed as a 'production aid' only, and is therefore not subject to periodic recalibration, must also be clearly identifiable to prevent its inadvertent use for inspection or test purposes. The use of a distinctive colour code is perhaps the best method of achieving this, rather than using tie-on or stick-on labels.

Q. What does "sealing for integrity" mean?

A. Measuring equipment containing devices which allow ajustments to be made must be safeguarded after calibration to prevent unauthorised tampering which may affect performance and invalidate the calibration status of the instrument.

Seals, or other preventive methods, should enable such unauthorised adjustments to be clearly detectable.

Q. What about other devices used for inspection purposes, such as jigs, fixtures, templates, patterns, or even test software?

A. Although these devices cannot be calibrated as such, they should be rechecked at regular intervals to verify their continuing serviceability, and appropriate records should be maintained as evidence of control.

Because of the need to use certified equipment, and the exacting requirements of equipment manufacturers' calibration procedures, many SMEs find it cost-effective to have their calibration work carried out by one of the specialist equipment laboratories accredited by NAMAS, or an international equivalent.

Further information on the control of measuring and test equipment can be found in *BS 5781 Part 1:1992*, which is recommended reading for all those companies who intend to carry out their own calibration work.

Chapter 6

Effective Quality Control Records

As has already been stated, records are the objective evidence of the operation of a quality system at all its stages. They are therefore required to be kept to prove the effectiveness of that system, and as such will be subject to periodic examination by the auditors and assessors of the company's quality system.

They will also be the means by which a company may support a defence of 'due diligence' if charged with an offence against legislation such as the *Consumer Protection Act 1987* or the *Food Safety Act 1990*. The defence of 'due diligence' is designed to balance the proper protection of purchasers against defective products with the right of suppliers not to be convicted of an offence they have taken all reasonable care to avoid committing, by offering proof that they "took all reasonable precautions and exercised all due diligence to avoid committing that offence".

Although under such legislation the burden of proof now lies with the defendant, he may not need to establish his case 'beyond all reasonable doubt'. The production of relevant records may be sufficient to persuade the court that the defence case is proved on the balance of probabilities. Whilst, at present, there is insufficient case law available to judge how the courts will regard the objective evidence of a supplier's documentation of an effective quality system in conformance to a standard such as BS 5750, the completeness of a company's records will obviously be a factor to be taken into account by the court.

Company procedures should clearly identify:

- What records are required, including pertinent subcontractor records such as material certificates/final inspection and test records as required by contract or purchase order. The mandatory records for evidence of compliance with BS 5750 are listed opposite.

- Who is responsible for their safe-keeping and ultimate disposition. Normally this would be the responsibility of the quality management representative.

- Where they are to be kept. Records can either remain where they are initially created or, after an appropriate interval to accommodate immediate needs, they may be removed for long-term storage in a centrally-located archive. In either case, due precautions must be taken to prevent unauthorised access, deterioration, damage or loss. They may be stored in any suitable form, such as original hard copy, electronic media or microfilm, providing that they are readily retrievable and remain legible.

- How long records should be kept. Between five to ten years is common practice. However, as the standard does not specify a minimum or maximum period, the management representative is advised to consider each type of quality record against the following criteria: possible product liability requirements; regulatory authorities' requirements; customers' contractual requirements; and certification bodies' requirements.

- Whether to use single copy or additional backup copies. Under certain circumstances, it may be advisable for backup copies of key quality records to be retained in an alternative location.

QUALITY SYSTEM RECORDS

ACTIVITY	ISO 9001 Ref.	REMARKS
Management Review	4.1.3	Should indicate scope of review
Contract Review	4.3	Should identify reviewer
Design Review	4.4.6	Should indicate participants and scope of review
Design Verification	4.4.7	Verification measures
Evaluation of Subcontractors	4.6.2	Should indicate scope of product or service available
Control of Customer-supplied Product	4.7	Lost or damaged
Product Traceability	4.8	Only when specified
Process Control	4.9.2	Qualified processes equipment and personnel
Urgent Production Release	4.10.1.2	Identification for recall
Inspection and Test Records	4.10.5	Evidence of compliance and the inspection authority responsible for the release of the product
Inspection & Test Equipment	4.11 (f)	Evidence of calibration
Inspection & Test Hardware and Software	4.11	Evidence of control
Inspection and Test Status	4.12	Identification of product and authority for release
Nonconforming Product	4.13.2	Concessions & repairs
Corrective Action	4.14.2	Investigation of the cause of nonconformities
Internal Quality Audits	4.17	Implementation and effectiveness of the corrective action taken
Training	4.18	Evidence of completion

Quality Certification for the Small Business: an IQA Guide

"I think we filed it somewhere"

Chapter 7

INTERNAL AUDITS AND MANAGEMENT REVIEWS

Internal Audit

BEFORE THE management team can formally review the suitability and effectiveness of their organization's quality management system (as required by clause 4.1.3 of BS 5750), they must first ensure that a comprehensive internal audit programme has been planned and implemented (as required by clause 4.17). The status and importance of each activity to be audited must be kept in mind throughout. The formal definition of a quality audit is:

> "A systematic and independent examination to determine whether quality activities and related results comply with planned arrangements and whether these arrangements are implemented effectively and are suitable to achieve objectives"
> *ISO 8402/BS4778*

One of the most difficult tasks for any manager is carrying out an audit of his or her own department. This is because we are all prisoners of our own experience, and see only what we expect to see and hear only what we want to hear. We tend to lack that degree of objectivity which is an essential attribute of an effective auditor.

It is important, therefore, to ensure that whoever is assigned to the task of conducting internal quality audits should be both trained and independent of the staff with direct responsibility for the various activities to be audited. Guidance on the qualification criteria for quality system auditors can be found in Part 2 of *BS 7229 — Guide to Quality System Auditing*.

Many small companies may find it cost-effective to engage the services of an external, fully-qualified auditor to carry out internal audits on their behalf. Auditors registered under the IQA International Register of Certificated Auditors would be suitable. However, this is not essential for compliance with BS 5750, providing the necessary degree of objectivity of internal auditors can be established.

Medium-sized companies may find that careful selection of auditors from a cross-section of departmental managers often improves interdepartmental understanding and internal communications.

To be successful, an auditor must develop the necessary skills required to identify the objective evidence of compliance or noncompliance with individual departmental procedures and work instructions, and through them with BS 5750. What exactly is "objective evidence"? It is information based solely on verifiable facts. Facts which the auditor has personally checked, has seen for himself, and therefore knows to be correct. Auditors must never rely on hearsay evidence or personal opinions.

If an auditor's opinion regarding the effectiveness of a particular procedure or process is necessary, then his or her own manager will have made this a clear requirement during the pre-audit brief. Unless personal opinions have been specifically required, the internal auditor must never express them, in the interests of good internal relations. Just stick to the facts.

Any auditor who is about to carry out an audit in a particular department of his or her own organization must be aware of how he or she is viewed by the members of that department. To them, the auditor is an outsider. (S)he will be coming into the department to find out exactly how they perform, to comment on procedures (or lack of procedures) which may be their life-time's work. A delicate situation.

The assessment could be carried out in any of three ways: by interrogating people, by going all out to find fault, or by quietly assessing the department against the applicable work instructions and procedures, in a polite and professional manner, with a view to helping the department achieve the organization's management objectives.

Internal Audits and Management Reviews

The third is the only acceptable method for trained auditors.

The auditor must seek the required 'objective evidence' of compliance and/or noncompliance by observing the actual activities and practices in progress at the time of the audit, by conducting a series of planned interviews with selected members of staff, and by verification of departmental records. In order to make the most effective use of the time available, the auditor must work to a predetermined plan.

Although a totally structured interview, using a check sheet of preselected questions, may at first seem to be attractive, in practice this method is best left to pollsters and market researchers. What is required is a questionnaire or list of 'memory joggers'. This should be compiled by the auditor after a detailed study of the departmental procedures, any previous audit reports which identify problems, and where appropriate the relevant clauses of BS 5750 and/or contractual or regulatory requirements.

The questionnaire is an invaluable document, but it should not be carried by auditors when in the office or on the shop floor. It is best used as an aid when planning the next hour's work. It is also useful when reflecting on the past hour's work, to ensure that sufficient random samples of work in progress and departmental records have been checked to be fully representative of the department's scope of work.

Experience has shown that it is best for an auditor to adopt a free-wheeling approach, and simply invite people to describe their jobs, their systems and the documentation they use. Pick up the points made and discuss them freely; then use whatever technique is appropriate to check that the actual activities are being carried out as described. This keeps the auditor on track, whilst at the same time it allows freedom to pursue a particular line of enquiry in response to observations and answers to questions.

Some typical examples of audit questions are listed at the end of this chapter.

During the audit, the auditor should be accompanied at all times by a member of the department being audited, or by another knowledgeable member of staff. This guide is required to assist the auditor in establishing facts, to facilitate interviews between the auditor and departmental staff, and to ensure that auditors do not unwittingly put themselves at risk through lack of detailed process or departmental knowledge.

What relationship should exist between the auditor, the guide and the personnel they meet during the course of the audit?
Auditors should follow these guidelines:

- Show sincerity and friendliness, earning people's confidence to encourage a free flow of conversation and understanding.

- Make the person being interviewed feel that he or she is the central figure, and an important person whose input is valued.

- Build the interview around the individual: his or her tasks, interests, objectives and feelings.

- Recognise your own prejudices and put them aside — in addition to getting to know the person being interviewed, we must also know ourselves. Everyone has prejudices, but by recognising them one hopes to achieve a better understanding.

- Be careful in giving advice.

- Avoid expressing opinions.

- Ask only one question at a time.

- Listen carefully to the answer.

- Listen to understand.

- Listen in a positive, attentive way so that the person being interviewed feels that the interviewer is eager to hear and understand every word.

- Listen in order to understand the other person's viewpoint: be sensitive to feelings, attitudes and motives.

- When listening, the auditor should respond in a neutral manner. A nod of the head or an encouraging smile will help to keep the interviewee talking.

- If necessary, repeat or rephrase something the person interviewed has said to ensure complete understanding.

- Use questions carefully, and allow the person being interviewed plenty of time to answer before asking a further question.

- Never give the person you are talking to the feeling that you are interrogating them.

- Avoid, if possible, asking questions that can be answered by a simple Yes or No. The question should make them think, and then explain.

- Keep in mind the well-proven journalist's technique of the 5 *Ws*:

What?	[Understanding]
Why?	[Reason]
When?	[Time]
Where?	[Place]
Who?	[Person]

    You can also add "else" to any of these to obtain further information: e.g. "Who else?" This type of question, together with "What if?", "How?" and "Show me", will always require the interviewee to be more informative.

- Avoid asking questions that only too easily could be misunderstood, or even upset the interviewee. The interview should be a positive experience for both of you.

This now brings us to the critical question of note-taking and the raising of the audit report.

If the practices observed or answers given are unsatisfactory, the auditor must pursue the investigation until sufficient factual evidence has been established to clarify the situation, within the time available. If a potential noncompliance is observed, all the relevant facts should be noted and verified with the company guide, for later discussion with the auditor's manager or team leader and possible inclusion in the audit report.

The auditor may find that a small notebook in which to record initial observations, comments and information is more helpful in maintaining a co-operative attitude than the use of a clipboard or pad of report pro formas.

There is no standard format for audit reports. Each organization's management is free to devise a format which meets its own specific needs. A typical example of an audit report format is given at the end of this chapter. Some companies may prefer to rely on a 'narrative' type of report which is circulated to all personnel with management responsibility in the area audited.

Never attempt to raise 'noncompliance' (or, as many organizations prefer to call them, 'corrective action') reports whilst you are in the middle of an investigation. Good report-writing needs thought and time.

Consider carefully who within the organization will receive, and need to act on, the report. A well-written report should state the problem clearly and concisely, and contain sufficient facts to enable the personnel responsible for managing the area to take timely corrective action.

Draft the report using, as far as possible, phrases from the relevant departmental procedures or system standards. This provides a disciplined framework for writing and avoids personal opinions, maintaining objectivity. It also helps the departmental staff to understand the problem and take appropriate action to correct it.

Remember that the purpose of an audit is to seek 'objective evidence' of compliance or noncompliance and to report accordingly. The atmosphere must never become hostile. The auditor must avoid appearing to be petty, pedantic or bureaucratic in the written report, and should address system weaknesses which need to be corrected, not minor, isolated instances of human oversight. Usually, the fact that the auditor has found a minor lapse of this sort will so embarrass the individual concerned that the lesson will have been learned and immediate corrective action taken. Nothing further is gained by including it in the formal report.

Only when internal audits are accepted within the organization as being totally fair and objective can management reap the full benefits. They must never be seen as a 'witch hunt' or a criticism of an individual's performance.

Management Review

In order to gain maximum benefit from the implementation of BS 5750, an organization's executive management should give careful thought to both the method and the frequency of their management reviews.

One method is for the management representative to circulate to all members of the management, with executive responsibility for quality, copies of the results of the internal audit programme (ref. clause 4.17), together with reports covering the analysis of processes, suppliers' and subcontractors' performance, service reports and customer complaints (ref. clause 4.14.3). Individual members of the executive management team can then formally comment directly to the management representative on the continuing suitability of the quality management system in implementing the organization's declared quality policy and meeting the declared objectives, and/or further corrective actions required. Alternatively, the CEO may decide to convene a meeting to discuss the reports and decide on actions to be taken. Either way it is essential that full records of the management review are maintained.

The frequency of these reviews is at the discretion of the executive management. Initially, whilst a quality system is new, it is advisable for this review to be carried out as part of the routine monthly management meetings. However, once the quality management system gains acceptance within the organization, the frequency can gradually be reduced, possibly to an annual review.

The requirements for analysis of performance (4.14.3), internal audit (4.17) and regular management review (4.1.3) are perhaps the most important to be found within BS 5750. Their effective implementation will assist senior management to achieve their objective of continuous improvement, leading ultimately to the goal of a Total Quality

Management culture.

AUDIT QUESTIONNAIRES

Examples are given of typical audit questionnaires based on the requirements of BS 5750 Part 1.

Requirement 4.3   Contract Review

1. Are all customer orders documented?
2. Have orders been checked for adequate definition?
3. Have any differences between quotations and customers' orders been formally accepted?
4. Who has confirmed that all aspects of the order can be met?
5. How were queries identified and resolved before work commenced?
6. Have repeat orders been compared with previous orders and any changes clarified?
7. Have all orders been approved as acceptable, and allocated an internal reference number?
8. How are order amendments identified, reviewed, and advised to all concerned?
9. Are all contract review records readily available?

Requirement 4.4   Design Control

1. Where are the documented procedures to control and verify the design of the product?
2. Are plans available identifying the responsibility for each design and development activity?
3. Are the resources and qualifications of assigned personnel compatible with the specified design and development activities?
4. How are the organizational and technical interfaces between different groups identified?
5. How is information between different groups transmitted and reviewed?

6. How are design input requirements identified and documented?
7. Who is responsible for the regular review of design input information and the resolution of incomplete, ambiguous or conflicting requirements?
8. How is design output documented?
9. Who is responsible for the verification of design output?
10. What objective evidence is available that design output meets design input requirements?
11. Who is responsible for the identification, documentation, appropriate review and approval of all changes and modifications?
12. What records are available of design reviews, alternative calculations, and/or qualification tests and documentation?
13. How are design changes controlled and documented?

Requirement 4.5   Document and Data Control

1. Where have the responsibilities and authorities for the review and approval of all documentation and data been clearly defined?
2. How do all documents available for use indicate who was responsible for their review and approval prior to issue?
3. How do the company ensure that documents available to personnel are the pertinent issues for their required task?
4. How are document changes/modifications controlled?
5. Who is responsible for ensuring that obsolete documents are removed promptly from all points of issue and use?
6. How are controlled/uncontrolled documents identified?
7. Is there a master list or equivalent document control procedure available to enable the current revision status of documents to be identified?

Requirement 4.6   Purchasing

1. Where are the records of acceptable suppliers and subcontractors?
2. Are the records up to date, authorised, and with an issue status?

3. Are any suppliers being used who are not on the list?
4. Do the records identify the criteria for approval of each supplier or subcontractor and method for periodic review?
5. Are all purchase orders definitive and, as applicable, do the details reflect the customer's requirements?
6. Where national standards are referenced, is the revision status stated on the purchase order?

Requirement 4.7   Control of Customer-supplied Product

1. What are the procedures for the control of customer-supplied products?
2. Who is responsible for notifying customers if their supplied product is damaged, lost or otherwise found to be unsuitable for use?
3. What records are available to demonstrate effective control?

Requirement 4.9   Process Control

1. How has the manner of production, installation and servicing been defined?
2. Where has the suitable equipment and working environment been defined?
3. What quality plans, procedures or reference standards apply?
4. How are the process parameters and product characteristics monitored?
5. What process control records are available?
6. Where has the approval of equipment and personnel been recorded?
7. Who has approved any criteria for standards of acceptability for workmanship?
8. What equipment maintenance programme is being implemented?

Requirement 4.10 Inspection and Testing

1. What quality plans or procedures are applicable?

Internal Audits and Management Reviews

2. How are products from suppliers and subcontractors checked for compliance with specified requirements?
3. What information is available about inspection or test by suppliers and subcontractors prior to delivery?
4. What statistical sampling plans are in use?
5. How are products released for urgent production purposes prior to verification?
6. What is the recall procedure if required?
7. Who is responsible for authorising dispatch to customers after completion of final inspection and test?
8. Where are the inspection and test records located?

Requirement 4.11 Calibration and Control of Inspection Measuring & Test Equipment

1. How is equipment permanently identified with a unique identity number?
2. How is the current calibration status identified?
3. Where is the frequency of equipment calibration defined?
4. How is traceability of calibration standards to nationally recognised standards established?
5. Who is responsible for calibration activities?
6. Who is responsible for establishing calibration procedures?
7. Who is responsible for the review of calibration results and initiating corrective actions, if necessary?
8. Who is responsible for the maintenance of calibration records?
9. What environmental conditions have been identified for the effective use of measuring and test equipment?
10. How are suitable environmental conditions maintained?
11. What environmental control records are available?
12. What precautions have been defined for the handling, preservation and storage of measuring and test equipment?
13. How can unauthorised adjustments to equipment be identified?
14. How is the continuing serviceability of test hardware and software verified?

Requirement 4.12 Inspection and Test Status

1. Where have the methods for identifying inspection and test status of products been defined?

Requirement 4.13 Control of Nonconforming Product

1. How are nonconforming products identified?
2. How are nonconforming products protected against accidental use or installation?
3. Who is responsible for the disposition of nonconforming products?
4. Who is responsible for the maintenance of the records of nonconforming products, including concessions granted and/or details of rework, repair and reinspection, or scrap?

Requirement 4.14 Corrective and Preventive Actions

1. Who is responsible for the co-ordination of corrective and preventive actions?
2. What records exist to demonstrate the investigation of nonconformities, and corrective and preventive actions taken?
3. How are the results of investigations and analyses advised to the relevant management for action, as required?

Requirement 4.15 Handling, Storage, Packaging, Preservation and Delivery

1. What specific requirements have been identified to prevent the damage or deterioration of the product at all stages, including final dispatch and delivery to the customer?

Requirement 4.16 Control of Quality Records

1. Where are the company's quality records defined?
2. Where are the quality records located?

Internal Audits and Management Reviews

3. What are the media used — i.e. original copy, microfilm or electronic?
4. What is the required retention time?
5. Are they readily retrievable and legible?
6. Who is responsible for the co-ordination of record-keeping?

Requirement 4.17 Internal Quality Audits

1. Where is the programme of scheduled audits defined?
2. Are these system, process or product audits, or a mixture of all three?
3. Have these audits been carried out on time?
4. Have all nonconformances been actioned within agreed timescales?
5. What training have the auditors received?
6. Have any unscheduled audits been performed?
7. Why were they done?
8. Has the audit schedule been reviewed for relevance and effectiveness?

Requirement 4.18 Training

1. Where are the training records of KEY personnel whose duties can or do directly affect the quality of the product? These should include (but are not restricted to):
   - Design & Development Staff
   - Laboratory Technicians
   - Special Process Operators
   - Inspectors & Testers
   - Auditors
2. How are individual training needs identified?
3. What are the external and in-house formal training programmes?

Great care must be taken to ensure that confidential records of individuals are not seen during the auditing of any training records.

Requirement 4.19 Servicing

 1. Where have the servicing requirements been specified?
 2. What control procedures have been established?
 3. How are service reports and records controlled and maintained?

Requirement 4.20 Statistical Techniques

 1. Where have the applicable statistical techniques been defined?
 2. How are results recorded and analysed?

A typical *Internal Audit Report* could look like the one on the opposite page.

INTERNAL QUALITY AUDIT REPORT

COMPANY NAME

Report No. ☐ Date:dd-mm-yy

Department: ☐

Quality Manual Procedure: ☐

OBSERVATIONS:

Signed:

Auditor:

Departmental Manager:

CORRECTIVE ACTION TAKEN:

Signed:

Departmental Manager:

Date:dd-mm-yy

CORRECTIVE ACTION VERIFIED:
Signed:
Auditor:

Date:dd-mm-yy

Distribution List
****
****
****

Stock Ref.No.********

"What's it look like, then?"

Chapter 8

THE ASSESSMENT & REGISTRATION PROCESS

WHAT IS 'accreditation' and what does it mean to SMEs?

Accreditation is the national mark of approval granted to certification bodies by the Secretary of State for Trade and Industry after an independent assessment by the National Accreditation Council for Certification Bodies (NACCB). The certification body has to demonstrate to the satisfaction of the NACCB's assessors its independence, integrity and technical competence against the criteria of the European Standards EN 45011/2/3. The scope of accreditation is clearly stated on the accreditation certificate issued by the DTI and is frequently described by reference to the Standard Industrial Classification (SIC) Code.

Under a system of Memoranda of Understanding (MoUs), it is intended that accreditation by the NACCB will be recognised in other countries which operate similar schemes. This means that certificates of registration issued by accredited certification bodies in the UK will receive appropriate recognition overseas.

A number of organizations in the UK and elsewhere which have not been granted accreditation offer to carry out assessments against BS 5750/ISO 9000. Although their fees may seem very attractive when compared with those charged by accredited certification bodies, SMEs are recommended to resist the temptation lest they end up with an expensive and worthless piece of paper — a certificate which their customers refuse to recognise.

The choice should be made with great care: the assessment and subsequent registration is not a single event. You are entering into a partnership which will continue far into the future. You must be certain, therefore, that you are going to be well satisfied with the arrangement.

Registration should mean far more than just receiving a piece of paper to keep your customers happy. It is the means by which you will receive, twice a year, an independent and objective report on the effectiveness of your quality management system. It provides a kind of 'health check' which will allow you to take any corrective action required to keep your business fit and well, and able to meet your customers' expectations.

You should therefore consult with your key customers to see if they have any preference among the available certification bodies. In doing so, you may find some purchasing organizations prefer their suppliers and subcontractors to be assessed and registered by the same certification body they themselves have been registered by.

You are, of course, free to choose in the open market. The NACCB maintains a directory of accredited certification bodies in the UK, with full details of their scope of accreditation.

It is wise to arrange a preliminary meeting with at least three of the appropriate certification bodies simply to get an impression of how they would fit in with your own organization. Compare not only the fees charged for the initial assessment but also the cost of maintaining registration.

Although every certification body will have its own unique procedures for assessment and registration, they all follow the general pattern outlined below.

Preliminary Assessments

Most accredited certification bodies will, at the request of customers, conduct preliminary assessments prior to the formal assessment. This is for the purpose of examining and reporting on the existing quality system to enable the company seeking registration to complete their preparations in the most cost-effective manner. A similar service can also be obtained from suitably qualified independent consultants, possibly at a lower cost.

The Assessment & Registration Process

As a preliminary assessment must be conducted within a limited timescale, because of economic considerations, the assessor will normally concentrate on the general interpretation/implementation of the standard against a previously defined and agreed assessment scope, rather than look for detailed compliance to documented procedures. The assessment findings are reported against each specific requirement of the relevant standard, e.g. Management Responsibility, Quality System, Contract Review. Where limitations on time prevent a particular system element or company department from being reviewed, or where there is no adverse finding to record, the report will always include a statement to that effect — for example: "The restricted sampling examination did not reveal any significant areas of noncompliance against this section of the standard" or "The time available did not permit review of this system element to be undertaken".

The report should clearly indicate the assessor's findings. However, comments such as 'satisfactory' will be avoided as the criteria are not as stringent as those for a full assessment. Any areas not covered should be referenced. Generalisations are normally avoided in preliminary assessment reports and noncompliance reporting should be restricted to the following:

a) clear and obvious noncompliances, supported by objective evidence verified during the visit;

b) observed instances of potential noncompliance where it was considered likely that more intensive examination would result in objective evidence of the noncompliance being found;

c) borderline cases, where the extent of any noncompliance may depend on the personal interpretation of the standard by the lead assessor during any subsequent assessment.

Note

The accredited certification bodies take every care, by means of training and monitoring, to reduce variability of interpretation of standards by their assessment personnel. There is, despite this, always an element of personal judgement inherent in the lead assessor's decisions.

The details included under each heading of the standard should explain:

a) the nature of any verified noncompliances, quoting examples relating to the requirements of the standard;

b) possible actions to be taken to correct the noncompliance, limited to a restatement of the standard's requirements expressed in terms which the company is able to interpret correctly and relate to its own situation.

Conclusions and Recommendations

Reports issued by accredited certification bodies' assessors normally do not recommend exactly how the company should resolve the reported problems. However, where guidance on the interpretation of the standard's requirements within a specific sector of industry is considered necessary, it is permissible to quote examples of acceptable practices as an aid to that interpretation.

In the preliminary assessment report, the assessor should comment on the following topics:

a) the practicality of conducting a full assessment, e.g. problems relating to the scope of assessment, complications due to multiple sites or the existence of shift-working, or health and safety and security considerations;

b) circumstances which may preclude any assessment resulting in certification, e.g. factoring, where the company may be unable to demonstrate the extent of the control exercised over the design and manufacture of products obtained from external sources, which are nevertheless sold to customers under their own company/brand name;

c) significant areas of verified or potential noncompliance and the possible timescale required to take effective corrective actions.

The report should clearly indicate the company's state of readiness to proceed with a full assessment, and contain any prescribed confidentiality statements in accordance with the relevant procedures of the organization conducting the preliminary assessment.

When the company considers that it is ready, and the initial application fees have been paid, the certification body will proceed as follows.

Assessment of the Documented System

Depending on the practice of individual accredited certification bodies, the review by the lead assessor of the company's quality manual and/or other relevant documented procedures may be conducted either on or off site. The perceived advantage of conducting the formal review of company documentation on site is that the procedures can be more readily related to both the requirements of the standard and the specific working environment of the company. This assists the lead assessor in gaining a better understanding of the significance of individual procedures. It is also valuable in the preparation of any preassessment questionnaires or check lists for use by team members during the assessment.

Particular attention will be paid to those requirements within the standard which include the phrase *"the supplier shall establish and maintain documented procedures for . . ."*

It should be noted that, whilst the standards state what should be done, it is the responsibility of the supplier's management to determine how these requirements are met. Reviewers are therefore trained not to usurp the prerogative of management in deciding exactly how each activity relating to the company's quality system is controlled. The reviewer will confine the investigation to establishing that the company's documented quality system covers all applicable requirements of the standard and relevant statutory and/or product standard requirements, e.g. codes of practice, which must be covered during the assessment.

The object of the review is to ensure that the company's quality documentation is available, in a controlled state, and distributed for implementation.

Documentation reviewed may comprise:

- the quality manual,
- departmental quality procedures,
- associated work instructions,
- company codes of practice,
- associated product specifications.

The reviewer will not attempt to assess the effectiveness of the documentation. This is the object of the later assessment, when implementation is verified. However, the reviewer will establish that pertinent documentation defines:

- what should be done;
- who is responsible;
- how the task is carried out.

Having completed the review, the lead assessor may stamp the documentation to indicate which documents have been examined. This is usually limited to stamping the relevant index, revision and amendment record pages. Stamping the documents does not denote approval. (In fact, the reviewer may have raised noncompliances.) It is merely a method of identifying which documents have been seen.

Planning the Assessment

The lead assessor is responsible for the satisfactory conduct of the assessment on the part of the assessment team. It is normal practice for the lead assessor to produce, in consultation with the company's management representative, a programme which outlines the activities to be covered during each day of the assessment. The programme should give specific times for the opening and closing meetings, and for each morning review meeting with the company's management representative or assessment co-ordinator.

In addition to the preparation of the assessment programme, the

The Assessment & Registration Process

lead assessor will discuss the following topics with the management representative.

Team:

The size and composition of the assessment team depends on a number of factors, including:

- size of company under assessment,
- product range and agreed scope of assessment,
- number of sites involved and locations,
- available assessment personnel with relevant experience.

Dates:

Wherever possible, the assessment should be scheduled as soon as possible after completion of the Document Review, including implementation of any corrective actions required as a result of noncompliance reports raised.

If more than two months elapse between review and assessment, any significant changes which have occurred in the company's documented quality system should be notified to the lead assessor before the assessment.

Hotel:

It is the lead assessor's responsibility to ensure that any necessary reservations have been made for the team. However, it is usual for the company to be consulted in the selection of local accommodation.

Arrangements for payment for accommodation will be in accordance with the appropriate organizational procedures.

Local Transport:

It is the lead assessor's responsibility to ensure that local transport arrangements, including visits to all related company sites, are clearly agreed with the company's assessment co-ordinator prior to the start of the assessment.

Meals:

It is the lead assessor's responsibility to make sure that the time available for assessment is managed effectively. The assessors may prefer, wherever possible, to have all meal breaks on the company's premises rather than to eat off site. However, due regard will be given to the company's facilities and normal customs, and allowance made in the assessment programme if necessary.

Use of Company Facilities:

Normally the only facilities required during an assessment will be access to a phone and photocopying services, together with a suitable base from which the assessment team can operate.

Availability of Senior Management:

It is not mandatory for the chief executive of a company to be present throughout an assessment, although this is desirable. It is important that the management team is represented at both the opening and closing meetings in sufficient strength to confirm the scope of the assessment, and to agree any corrective actions found necessary as a result of the assessment.

Whilst most certification body assessors will raise no objections to a company's consultant being present during an assessment, they will insist that the consultant's role is confined to giving advice to the client, not taking an active role as a substitute for the company's own staff.

The Assessment & Registration Process

Initial Assessment of a Quality Management System

The initial assessment of a company's quality management system (QMS) is a formal appraisal, carried out by an independent assessment team, to ensure:

a) that a documented quality system is in place which complies with the agreed assessment standard;

b) that the procedures described in the company's documented system are effectively implemented.

Conduct of the Assessment

All assessments begin with a formal meeting with management for the purpose of reaffirming the scope of the forthcoming assessment and how it will be conducted, and to agree any last-minute adjustments to the published programme.

Whilst it may not be necessary to go to the lengths of preparing a formal agenda, or taking minutes, the lead assessor should ensure that the following points are covered.

a) Mutual introductions should be made between the assessment team and the management team. Ideally, the management team should include the chief executive; at the very least, it must include the designated management representative.

b) The assessment criteria — the relevant part of the standard plus any agreed supplement — should be confirmed.

c) The scope of the assessment should be confirmed, together with any limitations or restrictions in relation to the total operations of the company, such as agencies or factoring of products.

d) An explanation should be given of the method of reporting adopted, which is for noncompliances, as far as possible, to be pointed out verbally as they are found. Adverse findings will be recorded by the use of noncompliance notes which will be presented to the management representative at the following day's review meeting, after being evaluated and categorised by the lead assessor. A clear explanation should be given of the precise meaning of terms such as *Major, Minor, Hold Point* or *On-Going Improvement*, used by the certification body.

e) Changes to the programme resulting from particular operational needs or availability of personnel should be agreed, and confirmation given that the programme covers all aspects of the agreed scope of the assessment.

f) A complete set of controlled procedures must be available for the use of the assessment team.

g) Confirmation is needed of the availability and terms of reference of company personnel who will be acting as guides to the members of the assessment team.

h) Office space, a telephone and photocopying facilities must be available, as required.

i) Verification is necessary of any special health and safety regulations which must be complied with on site, and whether there are any trades union restrictions which the team should be made aware of.

j) Verification is necessary that all company personnel have been made aware of the purpose of the assessment and requested to give every assistance to the assessment team.

k) The time, place and purpose of the closing meeting should be confirmed.

The Assessment & Registration Process

l) Confirmation must be given that all members of the team will respect the confidentiality of all processes and records seen.

m) An opportunity should be given for any questions.

Team Briefing

When an assessment team consists of two or more assessors, time will be scheduled in the programme for a team briefing. This gives the lead assessor and the management representative the time and opportunity to outline to the team members and guides such details as:

- the range of company products and processes;

- allocation of specific areas/responsibilities;

- the schedule for further team meeting/briefings.

Daily Review Meeting

Each day of the assessment should start with a meeting with the management representative at which the lead assessor will formally present and explain any noncompliance notes raised to date. Acknowledgement and understanding of the noncompliance should be indicated by the signature of the management representative.

Management representatives should sign a noncompliance report only when they are fully satisfied that corrective action is necessary to meet the requirements of BS 5750 and/or their own procedures. If, after further discussion, additional evidence is provided by the company to show that a noncompliance is not valid, the noncompliance note will be withdrawn and destroyed by the lead assessor.

Where a noncompliance note has been accepted and acknowledged by the management representative, the lead assessor may advise that the agreed assessment programme does not allocate time for reassessment and verification of corrective actions taken by the company. In this case, an examination of the actions taken will have to be deferred to a subsequent visit.

Closing Meeting

On completion of the assessment programme, the initial assessment is concluded with a closing meeting. A verbal summary of the team's findings and conclusions is presented to the company's senior management by the lead assessor. The presentation may not necessarily follow a written agenda, but should include the following:

a) Thanks should be given for co-operation and hospitality.

b) The assessment criteria will be restated.

c) A disclaimer statement will be made, pointing out that, although all relevant requirements of the standard have been assessed, the assessment has been based on a sampling of the quality system in operation. Therefore, where no noncompliances have been reported, it does not necessarily follow that none exists.

d) The overall summary of the team's findings will be presented, mentioning good points as well as those that require corrective actions to be taken. The lead assessor may at this stage invite other team members to contribute a brief comment, particularly if they have specialist knowledge.

e) Notification will be given of the team's proposed recommendation to the certification body.

In the case of a major disagreement between the company and the lead assessor, the company has the right of direct appeal to the certification body's senior management. It should be noted that the final decision in respect of registration rests with the management of the certification body, not with the lead assessor.

If the recommendation is that approval should be deferred, pending verification of corrective action taken in response to the noncompliance notes raised during the assessment, then it is usual for the lead assessor to discuss possible mutually acceptable dates for a follow-up visit, subject to later confirmation. Most certification bodies require this follow-up visit to take place within three months of the date of the initial assessment, or they reserve the right to require a further full assessment to be carried out.

A full reassessment may also be required if the management of the certification body considers that the number and nature of the noncompliances reported indicates an incomplete or totally inadequate quality system in respect of compliance with the requirements of the standard chosen.

Follow-up Visits

Where approval is not recommended immediately after an initial assessment, a follow-up visit is made. This is carried out either by the lead assessor, or by a nominated member of the initial assessment team. Its purpose is to verify that corrective actions in respect of noncompliance notes raised are being implemented satisfactorily by the company, and that the system element reported on now complies with the requirements of the standard.

On conclusion of the follow-up visit, the assessor will report accordingly to the certification body's management. The company's application for registration will then be reconsidered.

Surveillance Visits

Once a company has received confirmation of registration, it is customary for the certification body to carry out periodic surveillance visits (normally twice annually at approximately six-month intervals) to ensure that the company's quality system is being maintained in accordance with the terms of registration. Such visits may be unannounced, or may be in accordance with an agreed programme, depending on the practice of individual certification bodies.

They are normally restricted to a one man-day visit unless special circumstances require otherwise. Although carried out within a reduced timescale and scope, they normally follow a similar pattern to the initial assessment, including opening and closing meetings with company management, and any noncompliances being reported by means of noncompliance notes.

If the assessor reports significant instances of noncompliance with the terms of registration, the certification body will reserve the right to withdraw registration unless immediate and effective corrective action is taken.

Some certification bodies require a full reassessment to be carried out every three years, as part of their terms of registration.

Second-party Assessment

Assessments carried out by a company on its own subcontractors (second-party assessments) may also follow similar procedures to those described for certification bodies (third-party assessments). However, the following significant differences between second-party and third-party assessments should be noted and taken into account in the preparation of the assessment programme.

    a)   The direct cost of a second-party assessment falls on the company carrying out the assessment (the purchaser) and not on the company being assessed (the supplier or subcontractor).

    b)   Whilst the effective implementation of the requirements of a defined standard such as BS 5750 will be assessed, the assessment team will also consider how the manufacture of the product is controlled in relation to their own company's quality policy and contractual requirements.

    c)   Whilst the assessment team may raise individual noncompliance notes for action by the assessed company's management, the team leader may also be required to raise a more subjective and confidential report for the information of his own management, including recommendations in respect of current and future contracts.

d) The team leader may also have the authority to terminate an unsatisfactory assessment if there is objective evidence that the company under assessment is unlikely to meet the expected criteria for subcontractors. Third-party assessors working for accredited certification bodies would be in breach of contract if they terminated an assessment prematurely, without the prior agreement of the management of both the company under assessment and their own organization.

THE ASSESSMENT PROGRAMME

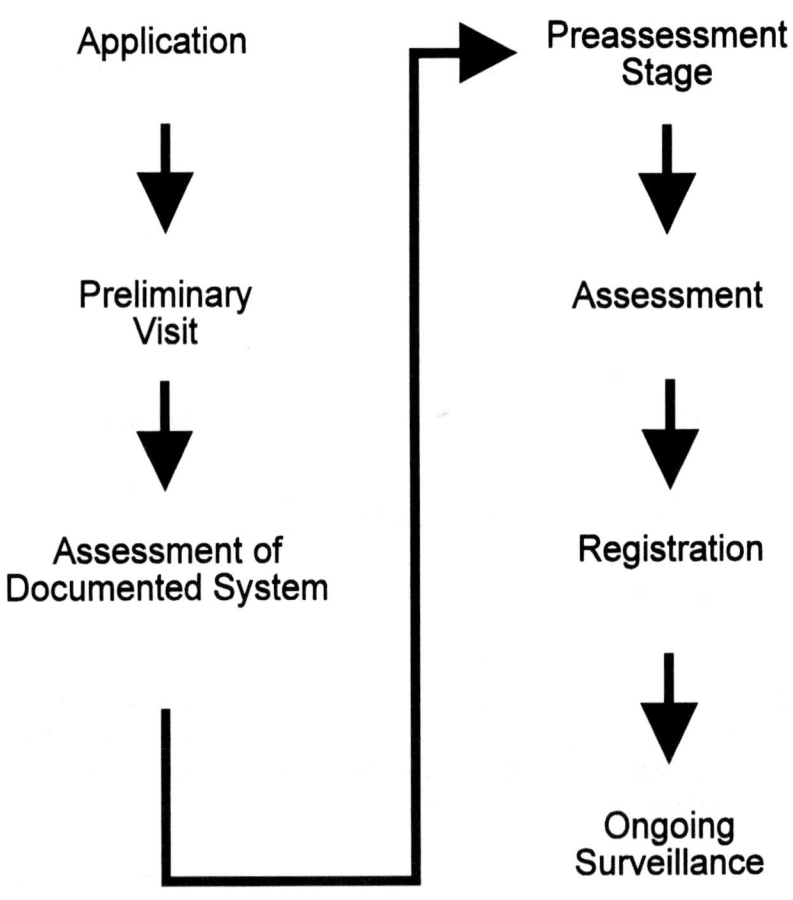

Chapter 9

PREPARATION FOR ASSESSMENT

GUIDES ARE personnel who are chosen to accompany members of an assessment team who have been invited by the company to carry out an assessment of its quality control system. This is an opportunity to demonstrate to a key client the effectiveness not only of your management of quality, but also of your quality of management. This is an important task, and the success or failure of the assessment may depend on the way it is carried out.

The following guidelines have been proven in practice as significantly increasing the probability of success.

Guidelines for Guides

1. Ensure that you are fully conversant with the actual working of the departmental procedures in your designated areas of escort, and how they relate to the requirements of the standard. If you have any queries, make sure these are fully resolved with the assessment co-ordinator before the actual day of the assessment.

2. Immediately prior to the assessment have a final check round your area, paying particular attention to the following:

    a) Remove obsolete documentation.

b) Remove unidentified material and components to quarantine for disposal.

c) Remove unlabelled/uncalibrated measuring and test equipment to calibration department.

d) Make sure all filing and record-keeping is up to date.

e) Make sure that authorised copies of all drawings, procedures, work instructions and specifications, including external standards such as national standards, are available where required at all work stations, and that they are clean, legible and the correct issue.

f) Make sure that objective evidence is readily available of compliance with standard procedures.

g) If computer software is being used for design, test or control purposes, make sure that objective evidence of validation is available at point of use.

h) Make sure that all work in progress is clearly identified and that its inspection status, where applicable, is known.

3. Make sure that you have received a copy of the assessment programme from your line manager, that you have identified your designated areas and times of escort, and that all key members of your department will be available when required. If you have any last-minute problems or queries, you must inform the assessment co-ordinator immediately. Remember, nothing is more important to the company than achieving a successful assessment.

4. Make sure you are on time for all your appointments, and that you introduce the assessor to the senior departmental personnel present before the questioning begins.

Preparation for Assessment

5. If the assessor asks a question which you know is not within the sphere of knowledge of an employee, you should tactfully advise the assessor of this fact.

6. Answer the assessor's questions briefly, courteously and truthfully. If you do not know the answer to a question, admit it and arrange to obtain the information as soon as possible. Do not guess or give your personal opinion. Resist the temptation to chat or volunteer information which has not been directly requested, and do not extend your answer into other areas or problems.

7. Remember, your function is to act as a guide; the assessor is responsible for carrying out the assessment. It is up to the assessor to find noncompliances: it is not your job to supply them. However, you must remain helpful and as professional as possible at all times.

8. If the assessor decides to complete a noncompliance report form, (s)he may ask you to sign the form as verification of the factual statements made. Providing you agree that the facts are in accordance with the incident as witnessed, you should sign the form as requested. Note that this does NOT mean that you recognise a noncompliance with the standard; you are merely verifying an incident.

9. Should you disagree with the assessor's written interpretation of an incident, you should politely state your reasons and decline to sign the form. If the assessor does not accept your explanation but pursues the point, note the written observation accurately, advise the assessor politely that you will have to refer the matter to the assessment co-ordinator, and suggest that (s)he also could refer the disputed noncompliance to the team leader for further discussion at the usual end-of-day meeting

10. Remember that you are neither authorised nor qualified to disagree with the assessor's interpretation of the standard. However, with your own in-depth knowledge of the department's procedures and processes you may, courteously, query the decision if you feel that the assessor does not fully understand the situation. An assessor can make mistakes,

and your query may save an embarrassing situation later. If you have built up the correct rapport with the assessor you should be able to discuss points without embarrassment on either side.

11. Under no circumstances should you argue with the assessor or allow yourself to be provoked. Remember, you are not adversaries, but professionals with a common goal — an effective quality control system. Never defend the indefensible.

12. Do not try to hustle the assessor. If (s)he is late for the next appointment, then it is by choice. However, do advise the next area's manager or supervisor that you are running late.

On completion of an area's assessment, advise the line manager and the assessment co-ordinator of the outcome as soon as possible, to enable them to initiate any corrective actions that may be required.

CHECK LIST FOR GUIDES

- Make a final check of your area just before the assessor's arrival.

- Know your departmental procedures.

- Know the assessment programme.

- Know your assessor.

- Be punctual.

* Be courteous.

- Be factual.

- Don't argue with or hustle the assessor.

- Keep the assessment co-ordinator and line management fully briefed.

FINAL AREA CHECK

- Has obsolete documentation been removed?

- Has unidentified material been removed?

- Has uncalibrated measuring equipment been removed?

- Is all filing up to date?

- Are all the drawings, specifications, procedures and work instructions clean, legible and the correct issue?

- Is the identity and inspection status of all work-in-progress clearly visible?

- Is objective evidence of specified requirements available?

- Is objective evidence of software validation available at point of use?

- Is everyone fully briefed?

"You've missed a bit"

Chapter 10

MAINTAINING THE QUALITY SYSTEM POST-REGISTRATION

FOR THE CEOs of many small businesses, achieving registration to BS 5750 fulfils their immediate needs. They now have that vital certificate to show to their customers and can get back to business as usual. Only in six months' time, when the certification body's auditor phones up to make an appointment for the first scheduled surveillance visit, will the CEO again start to take an interest in BS 5750. This, in most cases, is too late. The company has gradually slipped back into its old ways and the quality management representative now has a hard task ahead to prepare for the auditor's visit.

This is not the way to get full value from registration. The possession of a certificate of registration is the least of the advantages to be gained from compliance with BS 5750. The CEO and executive management team should view successful assessment and registration as the first milestone along the road to a Total Quality Management system. Their next set of quality objectives should be chosen to encourage their staff constantly to seek ways and means to improve customer satisfaction, together with continuing productivity and profitability.

The establishment of a sound quality management system, based on the requirements of BS 5750, will have given them three powerful management tools — if only they can learn to use them successfully:

1. CORRECTIVE AND PREVENTIVE ACTION

The company is required to record and analyse process and product data, internal audit reports, concessions, service reports and customer complaints, in order to correct and prevent any recurrence of actual or potential problems.

2. INTERNAL AUDITS

These should never be looked upon as a 'policing' activity on behalf of senior management. Their prime object should be that of a periodic 'health check' of the quality management system from which everyone can benefit. In particular, an effective audit programme will give senior management the necessary information to enable them to evaluate whether their current quality objectives are being met and, if not, allow them to take any necessary corrective actions.

3. MANAGEMENT REVIEWS

Whilst many demands are made of senior management, they must always find the time to consider the state of the quality management system. Review meetings must be held once a year, at the very least, and should ideally be more frequent, depending on the maturity of the system and individual circumstances. It is at these formal review meetings that the organization's quality policy should be re-examined and new quality objectives set, if desired. If the quality system is to be beneficial, management should always set objectives which lead to a programme of continuous improvement — making their people reach just a little bit further in order to achieve the company's revised objectives.

Management should never rely solely on the biannual visits of their certification body's auditors to detect actual or potential problems in the quality management system. However, providing the correct relationship has been established, this independent and objective overview can be of positive benefit.

The successful maintenance of the quality management system post registration should be looked upon as a team effort. Everyone within the organization can play a part.

MAINTAINING THE QUALITY SYSTEM POST-REGISTRATION

Note

The two British Standards on Total Quality Management

BS 7850 Part 1 — Guide to Management Principles

and

BS 7850 Part 2 — Guide to Quality Improvement Methods

are recommended reading for the senior management of all SMEs, if they really wish to gain the fullest benefits possible from establishing a quality management system based on BS 5750.

"It worked when it left us"

Appendix A

Glossary of Terms relating to Quality Concepts

The following definitions and notes have been extracted from *ISO 8402: 1994 — Quality Vocabulary* in order to clarify their specific meanings when used within the field of quality management.

Process: A set of interrelated resources and activities which transform inputs into outputs.

Note
This may include personnel, facilities, equipment, technology and methodology.

Product: The result of activities or processes.

Note
Product includes service, hardware, processed materials, software or combination thereof.

Entity: Item.

Note
The term entity includes the term product, but extends further to cover, for example, activity, process, organization or person.

Organization: A company, corporation, firm, enterprise or institution, or part thereof, whether incorporated or not, public or private, that has its own functions and administration structure.

Quality: The totality of characteristics of an entity (item) that bear on its ability to satisfy stated or implied needs.

Quality policy: The overall intentions and direction of an organization with regard to quality as formally expressed by top management.

Note
The quality policy forms one element of the corporate policy and is authorised by top management.

Quality management: All activities of the overall management function that determine the quality policy, objectives and responsibilities and implement them by means such as quality planning, quality control, quality assurance and quality improvement within the quality system.

Note
Quality management is the responsibility of all levels of management but must be driven by top management. Its implementation involves all members of the organization.

Quality planning: The activities that establish the objectives and requirements for quality and for the application of quality system elements.

Note
Quality planning covers product planning.

Glossary of Terms relating to Quality Concepts

Managerial and operational planning: Preparing the application of the quality system including organizing and scheduling. The preparation of quality plans and the making of provisions for quality improvement.

Quality plan: A document setting out the specific quality practices, resources and sequence of activities relevant to a particular product, project or contract.

Note
A quality plan usually references the applicable parts of the quality manual.

Quality control: The operational techniques and activities that are used to fulfil requirements for quality.

Note
Some quality control and quality assurance actions are interrelated.

Quality assurance: All the planned and systematic activities implemented within the quality system, and demonstrated as needed, to provide adequate confidence that an entity (item) will fulfil requirements for quality.

Quality system: The organizational structure, responsibilities, procedures, processes and resources needed to implement quality management.

Note
The quality system of an organization should be designed primarily to satisfy the internal management needs of that organization and should be only as comprehensive as is necessary to meet the quality objectives.

Quality improvement: The actions taken throughout the organization to increase the effectiveness and efficiency of activities and processes to provide added benefits to both the organization and its customers.

Quality audit: A systematic and independent examination to determine whether quality activities and related results comply with planned arrangements and whether these arrangements are implemented effectively and are suitable to achieve objectives.

Note
One purpose of an audit is to evaluate the need for improvement or corrective action.

Total Quality Management: A management approach of an organization, centred on quality, based on the participation of all its members and aiming at long-term success through customer satisfaction, and benefits to the members of the organization and to society.

The International Quality Standards and their BS 5750 Equivalents

As stated in the national foreword to the new BS EN ISO 9000-1 Standard: *Quality management and quality assurance standards, Part 1: 1994 Guidelines for selection and use*, the revisions to the standard have been made in the light of user experiences with BS 5750 Part 0 : Section 0.1 : 1987 in the UK (now withdrawn) and ISO 9000-1 : 1987 internationally.   This part of BS EN ISO 9000 was prepared under the direction of the Quality Management and Statistics Policy Committee of British Standards Institution, and was developed in the interests of international harmonization and international trade.

During the revision process, account was taken of the Vision 2000* strategy for the longer term development of the ISO 9000 family of quality standards which was adopted by the ISO Technical Committee ISO/TC 176, Quality management and quality assurance, in 1990. The following table lists the ISO Standards and their corresponding British Standards:

International Standard	Corresponding British Standard
ISO 8402 : 1994	BS 4778 *Quality Vocabulary* Part 1 : 1987 *International Terms*
ISO 9000-1 : 1994	BS EN ISO 9000-1 *Quality management and quality assurance standards* Part 1 : 1994 *Guidelines for selection and use*
ISO 9000-3 : 1991	BS 5750 Part 13 : 1991 *Guide to the application of BS 5750 :Part 1 to the development, supply and maintenance of software*
ISO 9000-4 : 1993	BS 5750 Part 14 : 1993 *Guide to dependability programme management*
ISO 9001 : 1994	BS EN ISO 9001 : 1994 (supercedes BS 5750 Part 1 : 1987) *Quality Systems - Specification for design, development, production, installation and servicing*
ISO 9002 : 1994	BS EN ISO 9002 : 1994 (supercedes BS 5750 Part 2 : 1987) *Quality Systems - Specification for production, installation and servicing*
ISO 9003 : 1994	BS EN ISO 9003 : 1994 (supercedes BS 5750 Part 3 : 1987) *Quality Systems - Specification for final inspection and test*

---

* *Vision 2000 — A strategy for international standards' implementation in the quality area during the 1990s.* BSI 1993

International Standard	Corresponding British Standard
ISO 9004-1 : 1994	BS EN ISO 9004-1 (supercedes BS 5750 Part 0 Section 0.2: 1987) *Quality management and quality system elements*
ISO 9004-2 : 1991	BS 5750 *Quality Systems* Part 8 : 1994 *Guide to quality management and quality systems elements for services*
ISO 9004-4 : 1993	BS 7850 *Total quality management* Part 2 : 1992 *Guidelines for quality improvement* BS 7229 *Quality systems auditing*
- - - -	BS 5750 Part 4 : 1990 *Guide to the use of BS 5750: Parts 1, 2 and 3*

Appendix B

Useful Addresses

Association of British Certification Bodies (ABCB)
The Coordinator
SIRA Limited
South Hill
Chislehurst
Kent
BR7 5EH

Telephone: 0181 295 1128

Association of Quality Management Consultants
4 Beyne Road
Olivers Battery
Winchester
Hants
SO22 4JW

Telephone: 01962 864394

British Quality Foundation
Vigilant House
120 Wilton Road
London
SW1V 1JZ

Telephone: 0171 931 0607

British Standards Institution (BSI)
389 Chiswick High Road
London
W4 4AL

Telephone: 0181 996 9000

Department of Trade and Industry (DTI)
Ashdown House
123 Victoria Street
London SW1E 6RB   Telephone: 0171 215 5000

or, for other parts of the United Kingdom:

    Scottish Office
    Alhambra House
    45 Waterloo Street
    Glasgow G2 6AT   Telephone: 0141 248 2855

    Welsh Office
    Cathays Park
    Cardiff CF1 3NQ   Telephone: 01222 825111

    Northern Ireland Office
    Department of Economic Development
    Netherleigh
    Massey Avenue
    Belfast BT4 2JP   Telephone: 01232 529900

Useful Addresses

The Federation of Small Businesses
32 Orchard Road
Lytham St Annes
Lancashire
FYS 1NY

Telephone: 01253 720911

Institute of Quality Assurance
PO Box 712
61 Southwark Street
London
SE1 1SB

Telephone: 0171 401 7227

International Organization for Standardization (ISO)
ISO Central Secretariat
Case Postale 56
CH-1211
Geneve 20
Switzerland

Telephone: 00 41 22 749 01 11

IQA International Register of Certificated Auditors
IRCA
PO Box 712
61 Southwark Street
London
SE1 1SB

Telephone: 0171 401 2988

DTI publications and videos on a range of quality-related topics are available from:

Mediascene Limited
Hengoed
Mid Glamorgan
CF8 9YE

Telephone: 01443 821877

National Accreditation Council for Certification Bodies (NACCB)
The Secretary
13 Palace Street
London
SW1E 5HS

Telephone: 0171 233 7111

National Measurement Accreditation Service (NAMAS)
NAMAS Executive
National Physical Laboratory
Teddington
Middlesex
TW11 0LW

Telephone: 0181 93 6311

National Quality Information Centre
PO Box 712
61 Southwark Street
London
SE1 1SB

Telephone: 0171 401 7227

Useful Addresses

"Quality? No problem"

INDEX

Accreditation, definition of 85
Accuracy, meaning of 63
Addresses, useful 115-8
Assessment 37, 56
    and registration process 85-99
    conduct of 93
    planning of 90
    post-assessment 56
    preparation for 53, 101-5
Audit questionnaires, examples of 76-83
Auditors 70
Audits, internal 30-1, 69-84
Audits, quality, definition of 69

BS 4778/ISO 8402 4, 35, 39, 69, 111
BS 5750, appropriate use of Parts 1, 2 and 3 7
BS 5750 Part 1/ISO 9001,
    list of procedures necessary to comply with requirements of 43-4
BS 5781 Part 1: 1992 64
BS 7229 70
BS 7850 109

Calibration of measuring and test instruments 61
    See also Measuring and test equipment
Certification body, selection of 51-2, 85
Closing meeting 96
Consultants 9
Contract review 16-19, 76
Control of nonconforming product 27-8, 80
Corrective action reports, composing 74
Corrective and preventive action 29, 80
Cost of assessment/registration 4, 10
Customer-supplied product 24, 78

DTI (Trade and Industry) 2, 9, 29
Daily review meeting 95
Data control
    See under Documentation and data control
Design control 19-20, 76
Documentation and data control 20-1, 77
Documentation, quality system 45-8

Documented system,
    assessment of 89-90
    implementation of 49-58
'Due diligence' defence 65

External assessments and audits 37

Follow-up visits 97

Glossary of terms 111-14
Guidance documents for quality management 6
Guides
    check list for 104-5
    choice of 55
    responsibilities of 101

Handling, storage, packaging, preservation and delivery 29

ISO 8402 See under *BS 4778*
Implementing the documented quality system 49-58
Inspection and testing 26-7, 79
Internal quality audits 30-1, 81, 83

Lead assessor's responsibilities 89-98

Management responsibility 13-14
Management review 75-6
Manuals 14-15, 35-48
Measuring and test equipment, control of 59-64, 79
Measurement uncertainty, meaning of 62
Medium enterprises, definition of 2
Motivation 49-50

NACCB 51, 85, 86
NAMAS 60, 63, 64
Noncompliance reports
    See under Corrective action reports
Nonconforming product
    See under Control of nonconforming product

Policy statement 39-40
Post-registration maintenance of quality system 107-9
Precision, meaning of 63

A unique anthology of the
TOTAL QUALITY EXPERIENCE
in British Industry and Commerce

Each chapter is complete in itself and offers the reader the benefit of its author's real-life experiences of introducing, operating and living with quality management systems. Contributions include:

- The role of TQM in the Management of Change
- Recognising the needs of the external customer
- Performance Management
- Employee involvement — a management view
- Employee involvement — a union view
- Quality costs
- The Consultant's view
- A management introduction to BS 5750

plus case-histories covering a wide spectrum of manufacturing and service industries, including Retailing & Distribution.

<u>Deliberately not a textbook</u>, **QUALITY 2000** is designed to share the experiences of those who have succeeded with those who want to.

Over 200pp in Hardback illustrated. Price £40 plus £2.50 P & P direct from
SYDNEY JARY LIMITED Publishers to the IQA
9 Upper Belgrave Road Clifton Bristol BS8 2XH
Tel: 0117 974 1640   Fax: 0117 973 7116   E-Mail: s-jary.co.uk
or send an official purchase order — you will be invoiced on despatch.

Preliminary assessments   86-9
Preparation for assessment   53-5, 101-5
Procedures necessary to comply with requirements of
  BS 5750 Part 1/ISO 9001, list of   43-4
Process control   25-6, 78
Product identification and traceability   24-5
Product liability   36-7
Purchasing   21-4, 78

Quality audits   *See under* Audits
Quality concepts, glossary of terms   111-14
Quality management, definitions of   4-6
Quality manuals and procedures   35-48
Quality records   29, 65-7, 81
Quality system   14-16,
    documentation of   44-8
    implementation of   49-58
    post-registration maintenance of   107-9
Quality system records, mandatory   67
Quality tripod   5

Registration, maintaining the quality system after   107-9
Registration process
    See under Assessment and registration process
Review of contract   16-19

Sealing for integrity, definition of   64
Second-party assessment   98-9
Servicing   32, 82
Small enterprise, definition of   2
Standard, requirements of   13-34
Statistical techniques   33, 82
Surveillance visits   97

Team briefing   95
Test equipment
    See under Measuring and test equipment
Testing
    See under Inspection and testing
Training   9, 31, 82
Training and Enterprise Councils   9

Useful addresses   115

xvix